Freedom from Family Dysfunction

Freedom from Family Dysfunction

A Guide to Healing Families Battling Addiction or Mental Illness

Kenneth Perlmutter

ROWMAN & LITTLEFIELD
Lanham • Boulder • New York • London

Published by Rowman & Littlefield
An imprint of The Rowman & Littlefield Publishing Group, Inc.
4501 Forbes Boulevard, Suite 200, Lanham, Maryland 20706
www.rowman.com

6 Tinworth Street, London SE11 5AL, United Kingdom

British Library Cataloguing in Publication Information Available

Library of Congress Cataloging-in-Publication Data

Names: Perlmutter, Kenneth, 1958– author.
Title: Freedom from family dysfunction : a guide to healing families battling
  addiction or mental illness / Kenneth Perlmutter.
Description: Lanham : Rowman & Littlefield, [2019] | Includes bibliographical
  references and index.
Identifiers: LCCN 2019015502 (print) | LCCN 2019017982 (ebook) | ISBN
  9781538121955 (electronic) | ISBN 9781538121948 (cloth : alk. paper)
Subjects: LCSH: Dysfunctional families—Evaluation. | Families—Mental
  health. | Families—Psychological aspects.
Classification: LCC RC455.4.F3 (ebook) | LCC RC455.4.F3 P475 2019 (print) |
  DDC 616.89/156—dc23
LC record available at https://lccn.loc.gov/2019015502

For my Jacquie

Contents

Introduction

My Experience in the World That Seems So Insane

> *The world we see that seems so insane is the result of a belief system that is not working. To perceive the world differently, we must be willing to change our belief system, let the past slip away, expand our sense of now, and dissolve the fear in our minds.*
>
> —William James

I first felt the fear in my family when I woke up in the dark to the sounds of my parents arguing. After a crashing boom (a lamp?), my mother's words tore up the stairs and filled my ten-year-old head: "Why can't we just make this marriage work?" Rocked to my core, I drew the only conclusion available to me: This is all my fault.

I figured out that if I acted in certain ways, I could keep the family together and the fear inside me would dissipate. When I was "good," there was less fighting, less leaving. If I got in trouble, that was okay because they'd focus on me and not fight. I also learned to keep things calm by not needing or asking for much. So, I minimized what I asked for or made requests in carefully packaged, camouflaged, or indirect ways. In time, I ended up cutting myself off from knowing what I needed. Getting punished felt better than when they fought or Dad left.

I was shocked to encounter the many ways this didn't work—I couldn't stop the fighting or keep them together. So, I tried figuring it out, sleuthing, or becoming Mom's confidant. "You can tell me, Mom." I ended up getting way more information than I knew what to do with.

I tried being broker and go-between and got blamed and used. Dad moved out, came back, then moved out again. Once I asked if he was going to leave. His answer was way more than I bargained for: "You know, I never had a father; he was old when I was born so I really only had a grandfather." I had no idea what to say but I pretended to understand. "I was an accident and my mother wore a winter coat in Brooklyn summer to hide the truth from the neighbors." I suspect I nodded sagely, but inside I was overwhelmed and terribly frightened.

At age fifty-two, I wrote this poem:

A Winter Coat in Brooklyn Summer

"I was an accident," my father said.
"My mother wore a winter coat in Brooklyn summer
To hide the truth from the neighbors."

We were alone together in the kitchen of our borrowed cottage
On the lake in Connecticut. It was before eight and I was very hungry.
You could see the American cheese bubbling under the broiler
On the faces of the English muffins we had fork split just minutes earlier.
You could see that red-hot broiler ring, too.

Soon I would be snorkeling in circles as was my custom.
"Stay inside the dock and the shoreline" (where it's safe?).
My bathing suit never fit right. I'm smiling in all the photos
But you can see the rolled-over waistband of my emotions.
Only rocks and the occasional angry-faced pickerel down here today.

We ate the English muffins. The cheese sticks to the roof of your mouth.
If you bite too soon it burns too; way up high—near the brain, I guess.
So much had melted that morning, maybe like Grandma's face
In the Brooklyn heat with her winter coat on.

I have come to think about wounded family systems as burdened by legacies of loss from which the members have never recovered. It could be the loss of a fortune or a homeland. It could be the loss of a child, a parent, or a pet. More generally, it involves the loss of emotional safety, the loss of freedom to be oneself, the loss of trust, guidance, time spent together, or hugs.

You may not share this sort of childhood experience. Yours may have been more dramatic and violent or more benign and ordinary. In any case, readers of this book share a set of feelings of powerlessness, responsibility, blame, anger, and fear in relationships with loved ones who require intensive help for substance or behavior problems.

The William James quote offered at the beginning of this introduction, written more than a century ago, accurately captures a truth about today's world, particularly by offering a glimpse into how to address the plight of families with addiction and mental illness in their midst. The insanity found in such family systems, to use William James's words, manifests as the chaos and unpredictability of life inside. Secrets, shame, and chaos saturate the family atmosphere.

This book takes readers on a journey to freedom from destructive cycles of codependency and powerlessness toward deeper connection to self and others. *Freedom from Family Dysfunction* provides a model for understanding family system turmoil and a method to guide families toward serenity, sanity, and wellness for the entire system. And it only takes one member to get things going. The process emphasizes creating connection and rebuilding trust by taking on a personal posture that feels healthy and sustainable. Specific techniques to do so are outlined. Maybe for the first time, safety, security, sustainability, and a happy ending will seem possible; and, best of all, the outcome does not depend on the behavior, recovery effort, or mental health of any one family member. It starts with you.

Beginning with a description of wounded family systems and their environmental characteristics in chapter 1, a gentle process will unfold to guide you away from the identified patient focus that has kept things stuck. You'll move toward greater self-awareness, compassion, and understanding. You will soon feel a healthy distance developing between you and the unpredictability, uncertainty, rigidity, and chaos of life in the family and its undercurrents of distress. Chapter 2 uses humor and metaphor to begin the journey.

Chapters 3 through 5 examine your personal beliefs and their sticky effects along with methods to question, interrupt, and disarm them. You'll find an easy-to-understand model of the wounded system and its destructive coping roles into which members are drawn and that repeat across the generations. You'll identify how the Stress-Induced Impaired Coping model, the term I coined for the condition plaguing all members of wounded systems, shows up in your family and how to shift away from its toxic effects. As your recovery develops, the condition will be interrupted both in your family of today and in future generations to come.

Chapter 6 offers a set of dialogues to bring to life a new way of communicating. Listen to the conversations portrayed there. You'll probably identify with the pain and powerlessness but quickly see how to change communication patterns to promote connection and avoid impaired coping.

Finally, chapters 7 through 9 provide specific techniques for your recovery. As these are embraced, you'll shift away from surviving to thriving as closer connections in which truth, predictability, harmony, and safety are restored. Some say the process has taken them from barely hanging on to finding profound meaning and connection, including to their true selves. Once this is achieved, they readily say, "I'm not going back. It stops with me."

Read on, skip around if you'd like, but try on some of the concepts and techniques. You may relate to some of the family members described in the various stories. Look for the similarities not the differences. Join me in overcoming the disorder, disconnection, deprivation, danger, doubt, and denial transmitted by our ancestors across the generations. Some believe, emphatically, it wasn't their fault; they were doing their best with limited developmental, emotional, and physical resources. There's freedom in seeing things this way. Or they weren't doing their best; instead, caught in the throes of their addictions or mental illnesses, they refused to seek help. Pain and loss were the inevitable result. This is part of the "insanity we see," as James calls it.

Regardless of the specific diagnoses of the identified patients in your system, the recovery process is the same, perfectly captured by James's words: *change our belief system, let the past slip away, expand our sense of now, and dissolve the fear in our minds.*

I wish you health and success as you step into the process of finding freedom from your family dysfunction.

Belief Systems

Uncovering the Wounded Family System

Whether you grew up in total chaos or an anxious, over-controlled freezer, you can free your system from the wounds of its past.

Sharon could just feel it in her bones. It was going to be one of "those" nights. Katie, her seventeen-year-old daughter, just got through the weekend and, miraculously, had kept it mellow. "She even studied a bit," Sharon recalled as she thought of how hard it would be to get Katie up in the morning even if she went to bed at a decent hour. Now it was 12:30 a.m. Sunday night and no sign of her. "Doesn't she know how important the ACTs are for her college apps," Sharon tortured herself, thinking, "This is junior year, everything counts."

It had become common for Sharon's mind to be filled with thoughts about Katie—her grades, her assignments, her schedule, her friends, her boyfriends (Ugh, that Darrell!), and lately, her comings and goings. "What does she do out there till all hours?" These thoughts circled in Sharon's mind as effortlessly as birds of prey rising on a hot summer's updraft.

Katie was a good kid most of her growing up, rarely causing problems. Then in the spring of tenth grade, almost a year ago exactly, Sharon got the call. Katie had been detained for marijuana possession: "Come pick her up or we take her to juvenile hall," the cop said on the phone. It turned out Katie would be suspended from school for a week, be assigned thirty hours of community service, and was mentioned, anonymously thank goodness, in the weekly newspaper's police blotter. A bunch of kids had a party and, to Sharon's shock, Katie had brought the pot.

Sharon could remember the conversations like they happened yesterday. Katie would be so cavalier, brushing everything off like it didn't matter and insisting this was the first time she'd smoked.

"But, you were *arrested*," Sharon said, "and that cop said you had brought the pot for the group."

"Mom, come on, all the kids were cited. We weren't actually arrested—that's when they take you to jail. Was I ever in jail?"

"Come on, Katie," Sharon practically begged. "Can't you see how this could become a bigger problem. I've told you your father's an alcoholic. It's in your genes."

"Mom, you worry too much. I'm running a solid 3.5, never been pregnant, or had an STD. What more do you want?"

"Pregnant! STD! Are you sexually active? You're only in tenth grade."

"Mom, get real. It's 2016. I know what I'm doing."

Things settled down for the rest of tenth grade, but that summer Katie was fired from her camp counselor job for drinking. Katie swore it was a single incident, and Sharon believed her. She held on to Katie's promises because they fit with what Sharon wanted: no more problems. "I just gotta get her through high school and into a decent college." This thought had become Sharon's mission statement, and she took some comfort when keeping this purpose in mind.

As it approached 1:00 a.m. Sharon felt the deeper terror run through her. "How is she ever going to get up in the morning? She has to do well on the test. And where is she?" Sharon reached Katie's voice mail for the millionth time and thought about calling one of Katie's friends. "She'd hate it if I did that. I'll wait a little longer."

Sharon must have dozed. At 2:47 a.m. she awoke to the sound of a rumbling engine. "Darrel's stupid hot rod," she knew. Peering through the blinds, she could see Katie in silhouette lit by the car's inside light. Katie had opened the passenger door and stumbled out after a long kiss. She fumbled for her keys, eventually opening the front door.

"Katie!" Sharon shrieked. "It's almost 3 a.m.!"

"Sorry, Mom," Katie smoothed her hair. "Darrel's car broke down and we waited like forever for a tow truck."

"Are you kidding me? You have to get up for the ACTs at seven!"

"Mom, I know. I was studying at Darrel's before we went out."

Was she slurring her words? Sharon couldn't tell.

"Really . . . what did you study?" Sharon demanded, knowing it had to be a lie.

"Like, everything," Katie mumbled as she took off her shoes, dropping them on the new white carpet and heading up the stairs.

"Wait. I'm still talking to you."

"Mom, it's 3 a.m. and I have that test in the morning. Wake me up ten minutes before I have to go, okay?"

Katie missed the first step, landing on her right knee, buffered by the new plush carpeting. Sharon could see what looked like bruises on the back of Katie's thighs as she fell forward.

"'Night, Mom."

"Katie, please . . ."

Some might call Sharon's family (including the one in which she grew up) "dysfunctional." Instead, I think of family systems with addiction or mental illness in their midst as *wounded*, and I have suggested my fellow professionals do the same. There are two reasons for taking this view. First, these systems are not *dys*functional, they function quite well to: cover up those things about us too terrible to face; limit or avoid emotional expression except for a few select emotions some members are permitted to express (like "Dad's angry"); avoid feelings in ourselves or our loved ones that are too uncomfortable or frightening; and, hold members in emotional and behavioral roles to promote a false sense that we're okay and reinforce the myth "everything's fine." The second reason to prefer "wounded" over "dysfunctional" is that it more accurately describes what's likely happened in the family: there have been past losses, setbacks, and traumas from which the system has never fully recovered. Often these were experienced by ancestors several generations back; their wounds and coping methods are genetically transmitted across the generations.[1]

Steve is a powerhouse father of three who co-owns a professional sports team. Silver-haired, always perfectly groomed, and a towering six feet five inches tall, he spends his days totally absorbed in his work. He'd been proving to himself and the world that he was nothing like his father, who'd left the family when Steve was fifteen years old. When Steve was twenty-nine, his Dad died of cirrhosis of the liver. In Steve's family of today, the "baby," Suzanne, always had everyone laughing. She'd wiggle her fuzzy eyebrows or put a crazy hat on, and for Steve all seemed right with the world. Then things got crazy. She started stealing alcohol from the house, staying out without permission, and even running away with a guy ten years older.

Steve doesn't like to think about how Suzanne, now seventeen, has gone to treatment in Arizona for self-harm and addiction. The invitation to attend the family program there got caught up with a million other things on his desk (playoffs were coming up!). When he realized he couldn't possibly attend, he sent her a new car.

"I just wanted him to come," Suzanne said, her ninety-five-pound body wracked with sobs. "I didn't want a new car, I just wanted him to come."

Like Sharon and Katie, Steve and Suzanne are members of family systems wounded by legacies of loss. When we examine such systems, we find a set of environmental characteristics that define the family climate. I call these "the dastardly Ds." In most wounded families, the atmosphere is saturated with these toxic features. They impede healthy development and promote coping in ways that make members sick. As you look over the list, consider your family of today, the family in which you grew up, and the family in which your parents were raised.

- Disorder
- Disconnection
- Deprivation
- Danger
- Doubt
- Denial

CAN A FAMILY HAVE A HEART?

If we allow the possibility that a family could have a heart, or a soul, or an unconscious, or a core (choose whatever sounds most appropriate), then couldn't that heart be wounded or damaged? Couldn't that soul be lost or off its axis? Or, couldn't that core be vulnerable or susceptible to illness? Whichever wording works for you, know that the system's level of woundedness shapes how members respond to stress. This involves both predictable stress (first day of kindergarten, grandparents' decline) as well as unexpected or extraordinarily stressful events (car accident, job loss, illness, or injury). Families with these wounded cores or hearts are susceptible to taking on the characteristics illustrated in Sharon's and Steve's stories: powerlessness, fear, uncertainty, control, intimidation, and feeling out of control. In addition, the members of the system learn to cope in ways that are both adaptive and pathological—meaning solving problems while making members sick. These coping methods are passed down across the generations and can arise spontaneously as a result of their epigenetic transmission. I have developed a model to explain this and provide the theoretical basis for the family system recovery plan this book outlines.

The model is termed "Stress-Induced Impaired Coping" (SIIC). It recognizes how all members of wounded families are coping with their experience of the system's distress and the toxic aspects of the environment. These impaired coping strategies also perpetuate the cycles of illness, loss, relapse, and pain and foster their transmission to the next generation. Steve and his daughter Suzanne are distracters. Steve uses work, Suzanne clowned around and became the family entertainer when she sensed trouble in the system, particularly between her parents. Katie's mother relied on caretaking to manage her anxiety by figuring out what others might need and how to fix them. Among the other members of the system there are escapees numbing themselves or leaving, like Katie, as well as blamed ones—scapegoats in trouble demanding attention and correction. Distracters, Fixers, Escapees, and Blamed Ones make up the four main impaired coping roles into which members are cast. The coping roles and their methods are explained in greater detail in chapter 4.

In the SIIC model, family wounds and losses, including those from past generations, have rocked the system and left it in a vulnerable, fragile state. As the alcoholic develops her illness from the consumption of vodka, let's say, the system becomes sick from the ways members deal with distress and uncertainty.

In addition to the dastardly Ds and the related impaired coping, the legacies of loss show up in several ways that keep families hurting: absent or unavailable caregivers; rigid and controlling rules or rituals punitively enforced; and violence—physical, verbal, or sexual. Many systems are plagued by substance abuse and addiction going back several generations. Denial tends to be universally present, meaning members can't let themselves think about and certainly don't talk together about what it's like to live in the family.

At the same time, please keep in mind that it is in these distressed family environments where we learned the lifelong lessons that shape how we meet the world, think about ourselves, and engage in relationships. As we watched our parents, their parents, our siblings, and our friends cope with the insanity they saw, we were shown how to cover up, smooth

things over, and conform. "Don't rock the boat," was a refrain we internalized and likely translated to "don't think about that." Many of us got messages that reinforced our sense of ourselves as defective. "Boys don't cry,"
"That's not what a good girl would say," and "You don't need that." Often
the messages were unspoken and left us believing we were wrong, at fault,
or too needy. When I overheard my mother plead with my father, "Can't
we just make our marriage work?" I was convinced, at ten years old, that
my needs were the problem. When I asked for something, I was either told
I didn't need that or got a shaming message that wanting it was greedy
or selfish. In other words, that I was wrong. In response, I repackaged and
disguised my needs, expressing them as indirectly as I could. During a car
ride, instead of asking to stop because I was thirsty, for example, I'd ask if
others wanted a soda, hoping someone would say "yes" and be the one
asking. When told to "stop whining" or crying, I could only conclude that
my feeling was wrong because my parent must be right. I internalized this
belief about being wrong and it controlled me.

These controlling beliefs about ourselves originate in a sense of being
wrong or defective. They lie at the core of what we must learn to change.

In wounded family systems, certain members appear okay and seem
to fit in while others become the problem. This encouraged a system
focus on the problem member and what's wrong with them. This person
shall be called the "identified patient," or IP. In an IP-focused framework,
the system overlooks its history and the effects of its operation. A disease-
model is adopted, similar to that used in addiction treatment centers. Yet,
despite medical advances in brain health (neuroscience), rates of addiction and mental illness are rising. The same occurs in family work: a "fix
them" disease perspective rarely works. Instead, everyone gets sicker and
Stress-Induced Impaired Coping is transmitted to the next generation.

Our work pays more attention to the system and how we participate within it. In this way, we interrupt IP-centered thinking and the
ways in which it keeps things stuck.

When you recognize the classic features of wounded families,
you're one step closer to *Finding Freedom from Family Dysfunction*.

LOOKING MORE DEEPLY AT THE ENVIRONMENT

When you recognize the classic features of wounded families, you're one step closer to finding *freedom from family dysfunction*.

Let's look at the Ds one at a time.

Disorder

"Look how great she is with Anthony," Angela's mother said, praising her five-year-old daughter's diaper-changing ability. With curly blonde bangs and a button nose, Angie, as they'd begun calling her, would come home from kindergarten and care for Anthony during "Mommy's nap time." Angie loved being called "second mommy." As her caregiving responsibilities expanded, her emerging identity coalesced around becoming a good mommy (including to herself). In a few years, she'd be covering up her Mom's drinking when asked by Dad and hiding Mom's Xanax bottles from her.

In this example, childhood development skews off course as key phases are skipped or prolonged. As adulthood approaches, a "parentified child" like Angie develops a false self with codependency at its core. She will likely struggle to ask for help and probably pair with unreliable partners—always expecting to be let down. Her explanation to herself: my needs are too much; or, others need me, so I must help out.

Twelve-year-old Jason spends his late afternoons with his ear pinned to the screen at his open upstairs bedroom window. He's learned to decipher the sounds of his father's arrival: the turning of the tires into the driveway, the opening and closing of the door on Dad's Honda, and the greeting (if any) his father proffers on arriving. Jason believed he could predict which dad would show up: Funny, loving, gift-bearing, jolly Dad. Sullen, withdrawn, gone-to-his-room-for-the-night Dad, or violent, yelling, critical, drunken, and terrifying Dad. Through this exquisite listening and predicting, Jason achieved a sense of control over the disordered and unpredictable nature of his family environment. Consider the effects on Jason's brain and skill development when so much of his energy was devoted to hypervigilance and trying to control the unpredictability in an attempt to create personal safety. Of course, he rarely succeeded.

Disconnection

A frail, gray-haired woman tentatively approached me on the break during day one of a three-day family workshop. Clutching her worn-out putty-colored purse, she hunched forward in clothes too big for her withered frame. We had been talking about loss in wounded families and the way family members can become disconnected from themselves and lose the sense of their fundamental goodness. "Dr. Perlmutter, I'm so disconnected I feel like I'm already dead," she said. Tears streamed down her face as she warily met my gaze with her steely blue eyes in their puffed-out sockets and added: "I just have one child left and I can't possibly bear to lose her." She cried after telling me her older son had died of an overdose the year before. These words went through me like a knife as I felt both her terror and her loss.

The disconnection found in wounded families can be profound or subtle. The mother in the previous paragraph had organized herself around keeping her children alive—futilely battling their addiction, self-hate, and shame. Having lost one to an overdose, she was gripped by the terror of losing her remaining one, now in residential treatment for addiction and self-harm. By focusing on this surviving child, she remains disconnected from herself; importantly, this protects her from some of the pain of her loss and powerlessness.

There are systems in which members have consciously disconnected from the system (leaving home at a young age, for example) or from another member (feuds and estrangements). I met a mother whose son went to Spain during summer break of his freshman year in college. Five years later, which included two rehab stays for his father and an older sibling who continues to live with the parents, he remains in Spain. He hasn't visited during this time. When I asked, "Will he be home for Christmas this year?" she replied: "Probably not, but his wife Maria looks so gorgeous in the photos he sends. We sure hope to meet her in person one day soon." In an unspoken way, it made sense for this Mom to make it all right in her mind for her son to be gone. Unconsciously, she knew he had escaped the family system and its alcoholic insanity.

This story, like so many found throughout this book, reveals the quickness with which members adjust to the wounded family system environment and its painful details. Using impaired coping, explained in later chapters, everyone is seeking to manage the sometimes intolerable internal experience of disconnection.

Disconnection also expresses itself in the form of disconnection from one's own self and sense of fundamental goodness, a sense of purpose and the opportunity to lead a fulfilled or meaningful life.

Deprivation

Recall Steve, the silver-haired powerhouse father of three earlier in this chapter. His daughter, Suzanne, wanted him to show up for the treatment center's family program. She had longed for his attention for years and with his latest absence, she reexperienced being deprived of the most commonly named missing thing in wounded families: time with Dad.

Spiritual and developmental nutrients feed healthy development. If we ask Suzanne years later what she wished there had been more of in the family in which she grew up, her answer will likely match that of thousands who grew up in wounded systems: time with Dad, attention, communication, affection, love, guidance, acceptance for who I am, and freedom.

I've inventoried this list with thousands of family members. Quite commonly someone says something like: "I wish I had been valued more for what I was good at rather than what they wanted me to be."

Developmental and spiritual toxins corrode closeness and connection. Wounded family members are deprived of safety. When asked what they wish there had been less of, the most common replies include arguing, drinking, violence, control, judgment, chaos, and blame.

Danger

I realized in my forties that I liked the TV game show *Jeopardy* because it mimicked life in the household in which I was raised. Saying, "I don't know" or misspeaking incurred an immediate and shaming correction. I got a message that I should *know the questions* even before they were asked! I made sure to avoid being exposed as inadequate or revealed as not enough. I learned to: (1) anticipate, decipher, or predict what was coming (exhausting and impossible); and, (2) avoid revealing that I might not know or understand (cut me off from learning). Anyone caught in these traps becomes unable to ask for help, guidance, or information. "You should know that," was the most common message. "I'm defective," was the internalized explanation.

To some it will sound exaggerated or overly dramatic to say life in wounded families is dangerous. For those in ready agreement, you know the pain of being verbally, physically, or sexually abused. These assaults on one's self, emotions, physical body, or sense of safety cause lasting damage. Some were exposed to physical harm in the form of slaps, spankings, or beatings. For others, verbal violence was more common, often including put-downs and name-calling. For still others, sexual violence was routine, including demeaning comments or jokes, intrusions on privacy, or inappropriate touching and looking. They lie at the core of relational trauma and can cause a lifetime of depression, anxiety, substance abuse, underachievement, self-loathing, and difficulties joining or belonging.

With these family dangers, it's common to smooth these experiences over in one's mind and minimize their impact.

It's important to note that this book and its methods are not intended to indict or blame our families of origin or our ancestors. Rather, we need to understand the forces inside us that inform how we've learned to cope with internal as well as systemic stress. In this way, we can eliminate SIIC and its distress- and disease-promoting influence.

Doubt

Dad announces: "As you know, Grandma broke her hip, so we can't go to her place for Thanksgiving. Your mother can't cook so we're ordering in Chinese and gonna watch a movie." "*Dad*! Do we have to?" the thirteen-year-old old complains. "Yes!" he barks. "But why?" the girl pleads. "Can't I go to Jessica's or something?" "No. End of discussion."

Doubt makes the list of "D" words because it captures the difficulty in managing uncertainty. Members are unable to tolerate the anxiety associated with not knowing what to do. They lack experience collaborating toward solutions. They jump to a solution instead of sitting in doubt. They get rid of it.

I heard about a single alcoholic mom who moved her high school sophomore daughter to a new state without saying more than, "We're moving." The daughter became anorexic within six months of the move as a result of losing the support and community she used to cope with life in her unpredictable and chaotic household. Years later, she learned her anorexia was a response to feeling invisible. She dreamed of a mother who would say, "Let's talk about how you feel about moving." She fantasized that's all it would have taken to spare her years of disordered eating, self-neglect, and codependency.

Doubt is driven by anxiety. When our ability to manage anxiety is impaired by fears of not knowing what to do or being exposed as inadequate, we are cut off from our curiosity about one another. Krissy came home after being dumped by her boyfriend. A bubbly, fun-loving, cheerleader type who preferred hoop earrings to studs and sleepovers with girlfriends to large parties, she had been unceremoniously dumped by her football-star boyfriend in the cramped front seat of his Mazda Miata. Running inside in tears, she blurted the story to her mother. "There are many fish in the sea, dear," her mother said. "Try a new hairdo and go to that dance Friday night. That should work." But Krissy didn't want a plan for what to do. She wanted someone to ask her how it felt. "That must feel terrible, I'd hate that," her dream mom would say. "I'm glad you're telling me about it," would have sounded like magic words.

Doubt and its anxiety intrude on our ability to be curious about family members' feelings and experiences. Believing we might be exposed as not knowing, we quickly fill in the anxious space with suggestions about what to do. "Why?" was met with "because I said so," Dad's classic cover. Many of us can picture such interactions and know the feelings that accompany it. "What the hell were you thinking?" wasn't really a question. It was a statement about inadequacy and foolishness laced with a heavy dose of shame. A real question, such as "How did you arrive at that conclusion?" or "Sounds like not your best thinking," or "What was going on at the time?" would have supported a more durable self and an ability to count on caregivers as safe. Instead, in most wounded families, the message transmitted was that we must avoid revealing that we don't know or are feeling uncertain.

Denial

Finally, our sixth D word is Denial. The denial in wounded family systems prevents us from considering or wondering about how the system operates. We can't say, "Well, Dad, I know Grandma breaking her hip throws a wrench in our Thanksgiving plans, but let's take a look at the options here. Maybe we could solve this other than the usual where you declare what's going to happen with no input from us, we feebly object and mumble some initial disagreement, then begrudgingly go along covering our misery during the event as best we can." Some of you are chuckling as you read this, identifying with the impossibility of such a statement coming from one of the children.

This type of denial goes beyond looking away or ignoring. Wounded family system denial is an unconscious process protecting members from deeper, more painful truths that can't be considered (without help).

Denial reinforces shame messages members internalize and come to be ruled by:

"There's something too terrible about us (or our history) to face."
"You're defective in some way you must never reveal."

Thoughts like these with their resulting powerlessness form the cornerstones of shame-based reacting—almost always found in wounded family systems. Shame underlies the need for secrets, cover-ups, control, blame and the resulting mistrust and mistreatment that follows. For the individual, a core sense of defectiveness develops that the person must manage either by numbing, denying, externalizing, or desperately attempting to control and keep under wraps. This is at the heart of true denial—wherein knowing oneself (or seeking to know) is experienced as threatening and accompanied by the risk of falling apart or being exposed. This combination of doubt and denial is a major stressor driving impaired coping.

Questions for Consideration

Soon you will have words to describe your family system, or what I call "the family deal." Take a loving and accepting view of yourselves, your families of origin, and your families of creation. Some key questions to ask as you move forward:

- What was predictable about this family? What could members count on?
- How was affection demonstrated?
- What was I valued/praised for? Was that different for others?
- How were crises managed? Key decision made?
- What happened during times of uncertainty or unexpected loss?
- What was prohibited from being talked about?
- How would I describe the system and its ways of operating?

WHAT TO KEEP IN MIND FOR THE NEXT FEW CHAPTERS

As you read further, think of yourself as a system observer. Go beyond focusing on the "problematic" family members (the addicts or ill ones). Shift your focus to examining the system itself: how it operates, its environmental characteristics, how members respond to one another, where power and authority reside, how emotion gets expressed, the nature of privacy and closeness, how members have learned to cope with the six Ds, and the effects of those coping strategies.

The next few chapters will guide you to a deeper understanding of the role you've played in your family and offer some images or metaphors that make it easier to imagine getting free. Next, you'll explore the psychological forces that have held you in that position despite the powerlessness you've likely experienced. Feel free to skip ahead to the worksheets or jump directly to the solutions, which begin in chapter 6.

A father attended two three-day workshops for healing family relationships with me. His family was riddled with trauma, addiction, and loss. Son of an alcoholic, he'd lost his mother to cancer as a boy and was now in a marriage on the rocks. His daughter, filled with hate and sorrow, commanded all the family's attention through alcohol and drug abuse, self-harm, running away, promiscuity that began in middle school, and refusals to get help. At the end of the second workshop in a session that included his daughter, he said: "I'm getting off the roller coaster, and I hope you'll join me soon."

• 2 •

Rodeo Clowns, Life Jackets,
and Being on Call 24/7

What Do I Become?

It only takes one family member to interrupt the family pattern and move the system toward wellness.

$\mathcal{A}$s discussed in chapter 1, our beliefs determine how we react to our problematic loved ones and the roles we take on in our families. One belief to adopt now: "I can change how I operate in the system much more reliably than I can change or correct someone else." You've likely wished something like, "If only she understood," when it's universally true you can't make anyone understand, believe, prefer, think a certain way, or be interested in anything. When you've been conditioned to influence how others act or think, you end up frustrated and disconnected from them and yourself.

Now, turn your attention to your beliefs and needs.

In the following chapters, you will take an inventory of the most intense emotions you experience, dig down to make a list of the various efforts you've made to change things (or change someone else), and identify a metaphor for the thing you become when family conditions are at their worst. You may be asking: "Why should I have to do that? It's her (or him) that has the problem. How are my emotions even relevant? I'm frustrated and disappointed. What else is new under the sun!"

Well, you're right. And this approach will interrupt your customary way of operating, which involves questions like: "What's the best way to get her to change?" "How can I get him to understand that he just needs to _____?" (Fill in the blank.) "Why can't she see that _____?" (Another blank.) Indeed, these are the right questions. The problem is the answer isn't very useful when it's you who's asking the question—even if you have a great answer, which you often think you do.

These questions and their answers are only meaningful when asked by the person to whom they directly apply—your stuck loved one. You've already given your loved one answers, suggestions, rules of thumb, lectures, money, and the truth as you see it. Over and over. The lack of success you've had getting this individual to see or to understand or to accept proves you can't be the source. This stuck person is either unable or unwilling to receive such from you. Unfortunately, before picking up this book, you've kept trying, believing you'll get a new or improved result. That's the insanity definition, right?

Well, this book is exactly about interrupting the insanity or chaos in the family system. Starting with you.

Think about Jerry: He's been retired from his corporate executive position for about two years. Married forty-one years to his wife, he wants to enjoy his retirement and his grandchildren. His daughter, Victoria, hasn't worked since she dropped out of college twenty years ago. Jerry and his wife pay her rent, utilities, and basic expenses. Victoria rarely leaves the South San Francisco apartment they provide for her. She drinks and says she can't go out during the day for fear her friends from high school will see her and know what a failure she has become. Bay Area rents have been skyrocketing. When Jerry does the math, he sees he cannot afford to keep his daughter in her apartment and have enough money for himself. His daughter's addiction riddles him with guilt and shame. His own mother was a drinker, something Jerry's father never faced. Dad smoothed things over and relied on hoping and praying as a way to tolerate his wife's eventually lethal alcoholism. Jerry blames himself for making the family move when Victoria was in eighth grade. She never stopped complaining about losing her friends in Seattle. Today Jerry sleeps with his cell phone on his chest in case she calls. He'll drop everything and go wherever she says she needs him—even with the flimsiest or most unbelievable of explanations. He acknowledges being angry at times, but mostly feels at fault and to blame. When he imagines insisting Victoria get help for her alcoholism, he has two thoughts: "If she went to rehab, I could close the apartment and create a setup that would be more affordable." That's thought number one. His next thought is "That would be devastating for her, and I'd be making her move all over again." Net result: he's frozen.

As Jerry and his wife explained their thinking, a crucial finding was made: Jerry believed that Victoria didn't fall into a classic alcoholic pattern, and therefore no substantial improvement could come from addressing her drinking.

"Victoria has ADHD and alcoholism," he explained insistently. "We have never figured out what percentage of her problems come from each one. Is she mostly an alcoholic or is it the ADHD which is the main problem?"

"So if you knew these proportions, you believe things would be better?" I asked.

"Yes," Jerry said hopefully. "Then we'd know what to do."

"Let's say it's 80/20," I said a bit playfully but hoping to make a point.

"Which way?" Jerry said predictably.

"You pick," I said somewhat provocatively.

A new truth began to dawn in Jerry's eyes. He saw how having this bit of data, this seemingly critical but chronically elusive formula, wouldn't help much. The idea that Victoria was 80 percent alcoholic and 20 percent an ADHD patient gave him nothing new. Similarly, if the reverse was the case, he'd be no closer to solving his problem—the exaggerated and hostile dependency (explained in chapter 5) plaguing his life. Jerry's fear about moving his daughter or causing her distress was the main obstacle to acting in *his* own interest. What were *his* needs? This was a question he and his wife were unable to ask, until now.

As Jerry dug deeper, he identified two roles he tended to take on, which can be described with metaphors or images. First, he would become the armchair psychiatrist, speculating about the proportions of his daughter's disorder: "How much this, how much that?" Next, and more saliently, he saw that, frozen by his guilt, he became inert, stuck, and unmoving. The image that came to him was of a life jacket.

"Yeah," he said with clarity. "That's what I have become. I'm like a life jacket. People really don't want to put one on unless they're forced to do so. They can't wait to take it off and throw it somewhere on the boat, usually in a puddle or under the seat. And I just lie there waiting for the next time I'm used."

We considered what he needed: A solution for his frozenness and a change in the financial deal with his daughter. He recognized how his past efforts to change Victoria weren't working. In addition, he was unable to notice how repetitively he was operating and what he was losing. He soon accepted that the answer to the proportion question would only be meaningful when it was Victoria asking the question.

He now dreamed of the day *she'd* wake up and say:

"Wait a minute. What the heck am I doing? I'm forty years old. I don't go out. I don't work. I have these two problems: I can't focus or get organized and I can't stop drinking. Which one should I solve first? How can I get help?"

It is only when troubled family members, like Victoria, ask these questions and seek answers that change becomes possible for them. In the meantime, until they ask that question, our task is to pursue changing ourselves.

When Jerry could finally say, "I'm not available to support this lifestyle for her any longer," the frozenness thawed, and he became less stuck. He committed to finding a setup for Victoria that wouldn't deplete his retirement funds. When he made this shift in his mind and refused to continue being a life jacket, the whole system shifted. Soon after Jerry's shift, Victoria was in rehab, the apartment was closed, and, after treatment, she moved into a sober living home, got assessed for ADHD, and found a job.

DISCOVERY QUESTIONS

As you read about Jerry, the things he'd tried, the forces that kept him stuck, and the life jacket metaphor, I hope you can begin to ask yourselves some questions such as:

- What have I tried over the years to change someone else?
- How have these efforts played out?
- What are the main emotions I experience on this ride I've been on in our family?
- What do I become, metaphorically, when things are at their worst?
- What is it that *I* really need for myself and my own well-being?

As you pursue these questions, you'll begin exploring what's going on inside you, rather than wonder about someone else's thoughts or needs. Looking inward will be in contrast to your long-standing habit of trying to figure out someone else's mind and life.

Notice when you're in another person's head. Make interrupting yourself when doing so the next step. In your mind this could sound like, "Whoops, that's her story I'm thinking about. I need to stop and come back to me." Try it as an exercise to see where it leads. Moving to here-and-now awareness could lead you to encounter some pain, regret, or traumatic memories. Building an emotional support system will be key to working through this. See chapter 7 for more. Practice catching yourself when you're inventorying, assessing, measuring, or questioning someone's situation other than your own. You'll soon notice how quickly your thoughts will jump to "them." It's okay. You're a beginner. Say something to yourself like: "Wow, there I go figuring someone else out again. Look how easily that comes to me and how strong the pull is to do so." Then come back to yourself. Take this up with a kind, loving attitude—a hallmark of mindfulness technique—since it will take a while to recognize and break this pattern. Focusing on others has helped you avoid emotional pain, especially powerlessness. It also keeps you from noticing how futile your efforts have been.

Mindfulness emphasizes self-awareness. It teaches how to avoid running on autopilot by increasing self-awareness and the ability to be present in the moment and in your body. Some helpful books to learn more can be found in the selected bibliography at the end of this book. You might start with Jack Kornfield's *A Path with Heart*, or one of the titles listed by Rick Hanson, Dan Siegel, or Jonathan Kabat-Zinn.

METAPHORS FOR STUCKNESS

In my many years of work with wounded family members, I've had the opportunity to sit with people as they encounter and describe a metaphor, or image, for the position they occupy when at their most stuck, most caught up in someone else's life and struggle, or taken over by the detail or drama of their loved one's problems.

Begin the shift from other-focus to self-focus by identifying the thing you become when the things are at their worst.

Here are a few examples.

Rodeo Clown

The rodeo clown is colorful, absurd, full of movement, and uses distracting as a way to manage danger—hallmark features of the chaos and impaired coping found in wounded families. The color represents the drama and high activity, the absurdity and jumbled movement capture the insanity. The job of distracting from danger parallels the family system's process of covering up overdoses, screaming matches, fights, sexual misconduct, stealing, and self-harm. Perfect conditions to send in those clowns!

Part of the rodeo clown's role, as in many of the metaphors, is to save the cowboy's life or at least minimize the damage. He does this through absurdity (his costume) by distracting a raging bull. At the same time, if you think about it, his job is impossible. A man dressed as a clown can't reliably deter a nine-hundred-pound bull from goring or stomping the fallen cowboy. But, when you get a couple of clowns to run around like maniacs, grab the bull's attention, and then scramble over the fence prior to being skewered, there's usually some interruption of the danger for the cowboy. Ironically, all this activity takes place to save the cowboy who was engaged in his own thrill-seeking behavior: riding bulls! Sounds a lot like addiction and the high-wire act that surrounds it in a wounded family system.

Siri

One Mom captured it perfectly: "I know what I become, I'm Siri. Stuck in an iPhone, waiting for someone to press the button. They'll mutter something to me. Maybe I'll understand it, maybe I won't. Then I'll give them something back which they may or may not use—I never seem to know. Then I get set down somewhere until the next push of my button."

Listen to her language. You can hear the frustration, passivity, and powerlessness. The sense of not mattering while at the same time being relied on and obligated to solve problems she might not even understand. Like Siri, she falls back on her limited set of responses, often not knowing whether she's helped at all. This experience of being called upon is extremely sticky because one is likely to repeat it despite obtaining little or no helpful results. It offers the Siri-mother occasional moments of hope that she can make things better.

These sticky forces reinforce classic ways of responding and I call them Goo-Promoting Factors, or GPFs. Caught in their gooey grip, the cycles of illness, relapse, and codependency repeat across the decades.

Oxygen Masks in an Airplane

Like Siri, the oxygen masks live in cramped, flat compartments, generally out of view of everyone else. Family members who identify with this metaphor describe its essential features: "I'm dropped into situations of crisis or emergency. I don't really understand the nature of the crisis or emergency; I just know I was activated. No one really wants me to show up; they're screaming and wishing I hadn't arrived. Sometimes it really is a life-or-death situation, though false alarms are possible. People reluctantly use me and put me on. They drool on me and can't wait to be rid of me. When it's all said and done I'm sprayed with some disinfectant and shoved back into my cramped compartment with three other of my fellows who offer me no comfort. And, I'm an ugly color, to boot!"

Buoy/Aid to Navigation

When the parent of a very stuck thirty-year-old came up with this one, everyone in the room related. "I'm a buoy out in the ocean. Chained to the bottom, I have no arms, just poke straight up and bob on the waves. Whether it's calm, sunny, windy, storming, foggy, freezing, or squalling, I'm chained there. I emit my tone and flash my light never knowing if it helps anyone or not. I'm at the mercy of the sea and the weather. Ships come and go; dolphins, whales, birds, fish do too, I guess. I'm held fast and soldier through whatever's going on, not sure what it's about or who's causing it. At the same time, I feel important—I might save someone from crashing onto the rocks."

Life Jacket

Consider the similarity between a life jacket and the oxygen masks. Despised and avoided yet occasionally relied on for life saving, these, too, are "an ugly color." If the life jacket could speak, it would say: "Many are forced to make use of me and they resent me. I'm bulky and unwieldy. Though people reluctantly admit I play a critical role, they can't wait to take me off. I'm often kept around to just be counted. I get shoved under a seat or into the lazarette and lie there in a puddle of bilge water and spilled soda. Eventually, I become moldy, thrown in the garage, and get thrown away. But you need me . . . you know you need me . . . right?"

You might feel sympathy for the life jacket. It struggles to convince others of its usefulness; except in extreme emergencies when they all madly scramble to put one on (or wish they could). The family member who identifies with the life jacket often feels undervalued and ignored, though convinced of their ability to help, a belief upon which they powerfully rely. Years of this leaves one feeling trapped and abused. Sarcasm, criticism, withholding affection, or making threats are often employed to maintain some power or dignity.

Receptacle or Toilet

When family members notice how their loved ones use them to get rid of unwanted emotion, they often contact a feeling they've avoided for a long time—of being a garbage can or receptacle. In this setup, disturbed family members use someone to relieve themselves of their anxiety or uncertainty. It can feel like being dumped on or thrown up on. I'm not trying to be vulgar or scatological, but the metaphor applies. A mother/daughter pair with whom I worked had been so stuck in this pattern that the mom made T-shirts printed with "I'm not your toilet" and on the reverse a picture of a large toilet with the classic red circle and diagonal line across. Once she recognized she was being used in this way and became more able to use her authentic voice, the mother refused to be available to receive these dumps.

I call these painful interactions "emotional evacuations." The stuck one contacts the family member and downloads their worries, fears, uncertainties, or doubts, often in a passive way. "I don't know, Mom, all these men just use me for sex. Then they drop me like a rag doll." How does a mother hear that? Well, probably with a large dose of fear and a small dose of anger. "Well, sweetheart, you're a good person, you'll find someone." Or, "The right guy is out there for you. You're smart and attractive." This has been said many times before and does nothing to change things. In fact, these "classic" responses reinforce the process that's taking place between these two: the daughter relieves herself of her pain and uncertainty by evacuating it into the mother, who absorbs and receives it. Unfortunately, the mother can't process the information in a way that offers her daughter much relief. The conversations conclude with the mother feeling filled up with worry and sorrow and the daughter going on to her next drink or next date. This condition can stay very stuck. See chapter 3 for more on the forces that keep things stuck.

Lawn Guy

A dad produced the lawn guy metaphor: "I'm the lawn guy. I have my big earphones on and I go up and down the lawn, mowing it. I can't hear a thing going on around me except the hum of the lawnmower. I know I'm performing a necessary function. When I'm done I look at my work with a sense of pride, though no one else in the house really seems to care. They complain about the noise. Then I get to do it all over again the next week." The lawn guy looks busy and feels important. He's found a way to insulate himself from the chaos or despair in the family around him. At the same time, he's marginalized and ultimately feels worthless.

Hula Hoop

Like the rodeo clown, the hula hoop is colorful and moves in crazy, unpredictable ways. It serves as a major distraction. People stop and seem fascinated by the hula hoop spin. Despite the high activity and flashy color, the hoop is hollow and empty at its center. And like the life jacket, when the user is done, it's leaned against a wall (often only to fall down in a breeze) or tossed onto the floor in the garage. Most end up in the dump after twenty years of hanging around the garage. Yet, when in active use, they command attention, serve to change the mood, and distract the user and the viewers from other goings-on.

COMMON CHARACTERISTICS/THEMES

Let's take a closer look at what these metaphors may represent or capture. More specifically, what are their common characteristics?

Use these questions to identify and describe the characteristics of your personal metaphor:

- What do many of these metaphors have in common?
- In what ways do I identify with any of the examples?
- How does being such a thing benefit the person who becomes it?
- Do I get used in that way or similarly?

Passivity

The oxygen mask, Siri, the life jacket, the hula hoop, and the receptacle are all activated by someone else's behavior. They are passive: idle, neglected, left, dropped, or shoved away until summoned by someone who's likely in a problematic or urgent situation. The plane is losing cabin pressure, Siri is needed to solve a problem, a bored teenager swirls the hula hoop, or a hostile dependent unloads into the receptacle. Think about where this leaves you: dependent on others and their need for you in order to fulfill your function. In such a state, you're hyperaware and on the lookout for others' needs and especially their distress. In this watchful state, your sense of meaning and purpose derives from providing the function you've been conditioned to perform. In turn, your sense of self will be tied to the frequency with which you get to serve and soothe your loved one(s) when they're bothered, anxious, uncertain, distressed, lost, angry, feeling abandoned, or alone. Wow! That's a really big job. It provides tremendous rewards for the self and keeps you coming back for more. Unfortunately, when the loved one no longer needs you in this way, you're shoved back into the box, tossed into the garage or a smelly boat locker, or idling inside an airplane.

Lifesaving/Necessary

Notice how the life jacket, the rodeo clown, the buoy, and the oxygen mask are associated with lifesaving, an activity of great importance. Many use lifesaving to form the core of a professional identity and sense of self. All activities that provide us with meaning, particularly at the level of life and death, will exert power on the psyche. As a result, one can be caught (imprisoned) in this position for a long, long time because it feeds an essential part of our sense of self and our innate need to be useful.

Functionality

Each of these metaphorical objects provides a specific function: lifesaving (buoy, oxygen mask, life jacket, rodeo clown), entertainment (hula hoop, rodeo clown), household care (lawn guy), information providing (Siri). The more an activity provides a necessary or important function, the more meaning one will derive from practicing it. When coping behaviors seem to provide an essential purpose, they make sense and feel meaningful, thereby making it possible to be held in their grip for a long time.

Distraction

Readers know too well the pain of life in a wounded family system. The recovery method described and prescribed in this book serves to relieve that pain. Consider the relationship between the sense of meaning your metaphorical position provides and the distraction offered as a result. Most of us will endure significant levels of discomfort or pain to provide a lifesaving service or help in a way that seems necessary. In other words, when offered the opportunity to fulfill our metaphorical function, we are distracted from the pain of the family system environment and its disorder, unpredictability, chaos, and seemingly endless cycles of pain and relapse. Notice how the lawn guy has cornered the market on distraction; he's in another world.

Absurdity

Comedians and authors teach us the power of absurdity to capture the human imagination, entertain us, and create memorable moments. In fact, one memory method relies on associating a thing to recall with something crazy or absurd or provocative, such as elephants having sex, or an explosion in the place where you set down your keys. Our examples of metaphorical roles all contain absurd or wild notions or images. Even the very idea that through passivity one could make a difference is patently absurd.

Take some time to identify the metaphor for the state you occupy when most activated by your thoughts about people you love who are struggling or mistreating you. See the metaphors question guide in chapter 8 for some additional help with this.

REINFORCING FORCES

Until we begin this work, most of us are held in our impossible positions (the metaphorical state) by a set of powerful forces lying outside our awareness. There are two sets of these forces: external ones that derive from the system, and internal ones tied to our core beliefs and personalities. In this section we'll look at the external or system forces that keep us stuck. Chapter 3 will describe in detail the internal ones, termed the "Lies That Bind," and offer you a way to uncover and then weaken these.

While it may seem arbitrary to separate these into external and internal, we do so to organize thinking and learning. Keep in mind there's considerable overlap, especially when we consider the role of perception. How one sees things is as significant to how they are experienced as the details themselves. In other words, there will be talk here about threats, losses, and covert messages (explained in a minute). The power of these is directly proportional to the meaning and significance one attributes to them. By the end of this process, you will be much more able to notice the effect of belief and perception and begin to question some of what you think.

Family member recovery work depends on interrupting the disabling effects of long-standing ways of thinking that reinforce traditional (classic) ways of responding. This is what William James means by "changing beliefs" (see quote in the introduction). Say you identify with the metaphor of Siri, the expert trapped in an iPhone. What might take place to activate you in Siri mode? Then what occurs to drop you back into the iPhone and its cocoon of silence?

Charlotte's mom's story will illustrate:

Charlotte just turned eighteen and she's heading out again with those friends of hers that her mother has never approved of. Mom's disapproval activates Siri talk: "Must you still see Janet? You know she was arrested last week and she's already had two abortions."

"Mom, please, I know what I'm doing."

Now in full Siri mode, Mom adds: "What about that nice Jennifer you were friends with last year?"

"Mom, I'm an adult now. I said I know what I'm doing. Stop worrying."

This has become Charlotte's common refrain of late, though just last week she needed her mother to rescue her when she ran out of gas.

Siri's effect creates conflict and corrodes closeness.

In response to the "I'm an adult" scolding, Siri returns to her little box of silence. But inside she knows it won't be long until she's again called upon to perform another rescue operation.

Sure enough, just after midnight, her phone is ringing. "Mom!"

BEGINNING SOLUTIONS

Chapter 7 will present the recovery program from Stress-Induced Impaired Coping. Here's a sneak preview of some techniques to avoid becoming the metaphorical thing that traps you:

Mindful Observation

First, begin by noticing when you're in the grip of the metaphor, that is, the moment you're aware you've become The Thing (the clown, the life jacket, Siri, etc.). Say to yourself, "There I go, I just became the lawn guy." Inventory the conditions that pulled you into the role. What was going on? What was said? What was true about your personal state at the time (tired, rushed, hungry, irritable)? Start to look for familiar patterns that activate becoming The Thing. For example, is it more frequently when she's been away for a while (or around you for an extended period), on workdays/weekends, when money is involved, when you're trying to do too much, or after you've had contact with another particularly problematic person?

This type of examination forms the basis of your emerging ability to interrupt yourself and sidestep or avoid becoming The Thing. Think of yourself as an anthropologist in your own family. You're looking around, wondering, and asking questions, not trying to solve things or "figure it out." As you move toward noticing and wondering, your perspective will shift and you'll be less likely to be taken over by a need to fix or control. When that fixer/controller need is activated, you're more likely to become The Thing, even if your Thing is passive and withdrawn.

Create a New, Healthier Metaphor

You've had considerable experience and become pretty good at describing what's wrong, what doesn't work, how people don't listen, and have a long list of "if only" statements: "If only he'd accept that he needs help. If only she'd respect herself more. If only my husband would admit he's an alcoholic." The list goes on and on. Part of the early work is to add a set of "if only" statements that guide you toward what you need and to develop the capacity for healthy, loving detachment from the details and the activity of your problematic loved ones.

Start by developing an "if only" statement that describes a position you'd like to occupy in which you'd be free: "If only I wasn't so taken over by his distress and problems. . . . If only I could give myself the things I want so badly for them. . . . If only I had superpowers to protect me from family insanity." Identify a metaphor for your preferred position in which you're strong, taking care of yourself, and free from being pulled into systemic insanity. In this position you wouldn't become The Thing; rather, you'd pursue an ideal. Here are some examples along with an affirming statement for each:

- Reliable father, available mother, empowered partner, benevolent leader, sought-out consultant. "If some of my family members can't make use of the good things I have to offer, I'll find others who will value them."
- Scientific researcher. "If only I could take a step back and take notes on these relationship patterns and classic interactions. Then I could think about and examine what's going on rather than jump in and rescue or explain."
- Peaceful planet: "If only I could be a peaceful planet in its own orbit and watch the other planets wobble and bob along. I'd hover above the fray and the chaos and check in with myself to determine what I need and what really makes sense for me to do."
- Free-wheeling ocean bird: "If only I could ride the winds above the ocean, no matter how turbulent the surface. I could create time away from this situation."
- Willow tree: "If only I had the strength, flexibility, and beauty of a willow, able to sway with the wind in peace. As of today, I'm no longer available to rush in, figure out, explain, and fix."
- Adventurous whale: "If only I could go below the surface and swim in the beauty of the deep. I know I'll have to return to the surface for air, but I'll be calmer then."

CHAPTER TAKEAWAYS

This chapter looked at the power of our beliefs to hold us in rigid, stuck positions in our families. We explained the term "Goo-Promoting Factors" to describe some of the interpersonal and intrapsychic (things we think in our minds) forces that keep us stuck. In our stuckness, we become a Thing that can be described using a metaphor that captures the futility and powerlessness we experience. Examples of these were provided. Lastly, we examined some of the forces that reinforce us in our stuck positions (more GPFs) and, alternatively, we identified a metaphor for a position we'd prefer to occupy in the service of detaching in a healthy, loving way from the detail and the drama we've been so consumed by in our problematic loved ones.

Chapter 3 provides a deeper look at the beliefs we hold that keep us stuck.

Looking Inside

What Keeps Us Stuck?

Stop making impossible deals with your loved ones by changing your beliefs.

Chapter 2 described the impossible positions and contorted shapes into which we are drawn, such as a rodeo clown or Siri trapped inside an iPhone. In this chapter we'll explore another set of forces that keeps things stuck: our beliefs about our problematic loved ones, what they should be doing, and our historical role in trying to straighten things out.

Kathleen and Will live on a tree-lined street in a lovely area featuring a community center where they play cards, swim, sample wine, and organize charity functions. In the last eighteen months, they've taken their daughter to the ER on four occasions. Twice she was near death because of her anorexia and had to be resuscitated as they watched in horror. Jenny, twenty-two, a golden-haired former track star, hasn't had a period since she was sixteen. Despite three residential treatment courses, she is now addicted to heroin and alcohol. Her parents have her living in their home after being asked to leave an eating disorder treatment facility for using drugs. Kathleen is confident that this time Jenny has learned her lesson and will find and keep a job. While Jenny sleeps most of the day, Kathleen scours the online ads for job leads and is editing a new version of Jenny's résumé.

Kathleen's belief that Jenny could walk away from heroin and alcohol to obtain and keep a job has been proven to be entirely unrealistic. Nonetheless, Kathleen will stick to her story that Jenny can do so. Her belief, "She'll do it this time," traps her in the impossible position she has occupied for ten years. This story, like the other "Lies That Bind," drags a person toward the metaphorical positions explained in chapter 2. Their magnetic power blinds us to the painful truth of our powerlessness while gluing us to the indefinite repetition of the patterns of the past.

Here are the most common:

- "I'm keeping him/her alive"
- "If only I . . ."
- "I owe"
- "I can't stand his/her discomfort"
- "S/he'll relapse if I . . ."

These beliefs drive our classic responses to the problematic behaviors of our loved ones. These patterned responses perpetuate the distress in the family system. Everyone plays a part in the family drama as members cope as best they can with their experience of the wounded system environment (see the six Ds described in chapter 1). Some family members seem immune or unaffected. They drive you crazy, right? You're busy in a whirlwind of action intended to keep everything working and everyone "happy," yet some members bumble along like nothing's wrong: they minimize, they criticize you for "overreacting," and they may occasionally blow up or disappear. These detached members are in their own story, too, and their ways of responding, just like compulsive fixing, fuel Stress-Induced Impaired Coping (SIIC), the term explained in chapter 1 for the condition that affects all members of dysfunctional families.

For too long, we've pursued solutions for our powerlessness and fear by trying to change (improve or make healthy) our problematic loved ones. At what point can we conclude we will not be successful at changing them? Well, I hope that point for you is *now*. I have worked with parents who've come to me when their "kids" are forty, forty-five, fifty, and fifty-five years old. Often, these parents are in the same jam they were in when the kid was seventeen. Please learn from them and do this work to interrupt the stuck patterns and find *freedom from family dysfunction*.

Let's look at these Lies That Bind. Later in this chapter you'll find some questions to help you identify the story that grips you. Explore the power and influence the story has on you and the system. This chapter concludes with ways to reduce their power and "gooeyness."

"I'M KEEPING HIM/HER ALIVE"

This is the most common, the most painful, and frequently all-consuming belief. It can invade and take over the mind of a parent or spouse, freezing one into repetitive serving and soothing, in turn reinforcing the cycles of exaggerated and hostile dependency (explained more in chapter 5). When your daughter puts her life, freedom, safety, or future at risk, as so many with addiction, mood problems, or disordered eating will do, our fear tells us if we say "no," or hold a limit, or act in our self-interest, our loved one will die. Or we worry they'll leave, never speak to us again, or become homeless and end up in prison. "I'll lose her forever" becomes the lie's form.

The thought of losing a loved one, particularly a child (of any age), is terrifying. Fears of such loss are magnified over the years, made more real by the risky behaviors and actual losses your loved ones encounter—hospitalization, overdose, disappearance, or arrest.

So, What's the Lie? Identifying the Distortion

When asked, most loved ones will readily agree they have put their lives, freedom, and futures at risk by their behaviors (substance abuse, suicidal thinking/planning, high-risk sexual or criminal activity). But it's their answer to the next question that reveals the lie:

"When it comes to possibly losing your life/freedom because of your condition, can your mother/father/spouse prevent that?" In every case, the person says "no." This is difficult for family members to accept, especially if there have been times when the family has saved this person or gotten them to safety. Like the time when Debby, a finance manager at a bank, suspected her sixteen-year-old, Skyler, was cutting herself at her boyfriend's house. After receiving an odd and cryptic text message from her, Debby pushed past the crew of boys partying while the parents were away to find her daughter passed out in the upstairs bathroom. Skyler was resuscitated by EMTs and received more than twenty-five stitches. Debby came away stunned by her awareness that she'd saved Skyler's life.

Such an event formed a powerfully reinforcing memory in Debby's mind, cementing the belief "I'm keeping her alive." But, when we ask whether Debby can *reliably* keep Skyler alive, meaning day and night, seven days a week, the answer must be "no." Certainly if we ask Skyler this question, she will echo the truth that Debby, or anyone else for that matter, cannot reliably keep her alive or protected. So, if you believe you're keeping someone alive or able to prevent them from incurring further dreadful losses, and they would tell you that you can't reliably do so, the belief "I'm keeping her alive" is proven to be a lie. You have believed it to avoid facing the powerlessness and associated terror that would follow.

For fixers of all varieties, powerlessness is the least desirable state. Ideas such as "Something can be done," or "I'll never give up," or "Where there's a will, there's a way" fuel soldiering on.

At the same time, if you're responding based on a distorted belief, or lie, frustration and powerlessness will be the inevitable and awful result. Freedom from this state requires recognizing and then letting go of the parts of the story containing the distortions. While you *can* be free of the lie's grip, you will need additional help to deal with the fear of loss, which is what the lie protected you from. That fear may never go away entirely.

This chapter will explain how once the lie is named, you can shift away from chasing it toward facing the parts of it that are untrue. You'll then be at less risk of being taken over by it and working to solve an unsolvable problem. In "I'm keeping him alive," the awful truth is that you could lose this person—a tragedy from which there is never full recovery. In that position, intense feelings of powerlessness, loss, and even rage may emerge. Shifting the focus to managing those feelings, rather than trying to keep the story afloat, loosens the lie's grip.

Now let's look at:

"IF ONLY I . . ."

The "if only" lie is powerful and compelling. It comes in two forms: the regret form ("If only I hadn't . . .") and the aspirational form ("If only I can . . .").

In regret mode, you believe "If only I hadn't" gotten divorced, married that person, moved, changed jobs, worked nights, listened to that doctor, and so on, then things wouldn't be as they are. This is a blame-filled, shame-driven set of beliefs that can keep one very stuck. It ties directly into the next lie, described below: "I owe."

The aspirational form of "if only" involves hope and sounds like: "If only I can find" the right psychiatrist, medication, treatment center, food program or diet, tattoo removal parlor, living situation, course of study, volunteer job, boyfriend, girlfriend, rescue animal, hobby, or source of meaning for her, then things would get better (and I'd be relieved of my misery). This is a powerful notion: When engaged in the research, you feel a sense of purpose and meaning. This distraction can be quite relieving, particularly in contrast to the powerlessness experienced when seeing how stuck your loved one can be. Remember Jenny, described above, kicked out of treatment for using? Her mother, Kathleen, spent the early days when Jenny was back in her home researching job opportunities for her daughter. It is likely Kathleen felt energized and more hopeful when engaged in such a task. Unfortunately, Jenny was asleep upstairs.

So, What's the Lie? Identifying the Distortion

The two "if only" stories can be debunked as follows: For the regret version, it isn't possible to change the past; regret breeds rumination and repetition. In essence, the lie involves believing this way of thinking is useful. When we hold on to the losses and traumas from the past, we're much more likely to be hampered in our efforts to make changes to anyone, including ourselves, in the present. Of course, the idea of changing yourself is a new one; however, that's at the core of family system recovery—embracing what you need to address and change. As with so many of the forces we've examined thus far, regret keeps things stuck and perpetuates the cycles of pain and loss.

In the aspirational version, "If only I find . . . ," the evidence shows there isn't one thing that is going to remedy your loved one's situation. In addition, trying to figure out what loved ones may need or should do has the following adverse effects and distortions:

- It tells them you don't believe they know what's best for themselves and that they can't figure it out.
- It assumes they believe you could provide answers for them. They probably don't believe that; instead, they may see you as meddling, misunderstanding, and judging them. They are unlikely to embrace or take up even your best suggestions and solutions.

- To continue searching in "if only" mode overlooks the way your efforts have failed thus far. Complete the "What I've Tried" worksheet in chapter 8 to open your eyes a bit wider about the futility of "If only I can find . . ."

As in all the lies that bind, "If only I can find" provides relief from powerlessness, in this case a sense of purpose and illusion of control. While this offers temporary comfort and may camouflage your powerlessness, it reinforces and deepens the goo by holding the system in the Identified Patient setup. This is your work to interrupt.

The next story is labeled:

"I OWE"

Andrea's daughter Cyndi has been out of control for nearly two years, and she's only sixteen. Cyndi cuts school, is always late, and hangs out with unsavory older boys who, to Andrea, look like grown men. Andrea, a single mom, has worried Cyndi has been having sex since age fourteen. Despite sending Cyndi to wilderness treatment about a year ago, this last school year has been off the rails: daily calls from school about missed classes, two arrests for alcohol possession or drunk in public. Now Cyndi's on juvenile probation (although the probation people don't seem to be doing anything) for shoplifting. She's still smoking pot daily, staying out way past curfew, and lying about nearly everything. Andrea has a therapist who tells her to "set limits" and "put self-care first" but she just can't bear to say "no." Cyndi says that being "sent away was the worst thing that ever happened" to her. Worst of all, Andrea is plagued by a nagging belief that during the two years they lived with Andrea's second husband, Chuck, when Cyndi was eleven to thirteen, he may have behaved sexually toward Cyndi. Andrea once believed she'd seen him photographing Cyndi as she came out of the shower. He insisted he wasn't and, of course, Andrea wanted to believe him. Although Cyndi denied she had been touched or harmed in any way, she always called him "the Creep." The breakup was very messy with Chuck, who, one night after they split up, sat in his car outside the house texting furiously to be let in and morosely played "their song" over and over on his car stereo until a neighbor threatened to call the police.

Now, seeing Cyndi off the rails, Andrea questions whether Chuck harmed her. Did he touch her, spy on her, or make things feel unsafe for her? Therapists at the wilderness program thought Cyndi's troubles could be linked to sexual abuse, but nothing concrete was discovered. They also said Cyndi should go to therapeutic boarding school and not return home to her circle of friends and drug contacts. But, Andrea couldn't bear Cyndi's pleas to come home and "be together, Mommy, you and me like it's supposed to be." Now Andrea wished she had listened and enrolled her daughter in the long-term treatment. "Will I ever have any peace?" Andrea frequently thought, though guilty feelings and fears quickly intruded. "This is all my fault" became the unshakeable core belief ruling her thoughts about her situation with her daughter.

To some readers this will seem an extreme example; to others it will sound less severe than the situation you may be facing. Cyndi's out-of-control behavior and the parental challenges it poses sit well above average, though not off the charts. Andrea's powerlessness is common, made more difficult by her position as a single mother. The story illustrates that Andrea's powerlessness over her daughter's behavior and inability to set limits or seek help are reinforced by Andrea's guilt and self-blame. Believing "it's all my fault" keeps things really stuck. Andrea can't help but use serving and soothing, rather than help seeking or limit setting, in response to Cyndi's various demands and predicaments. Andrea becomes persuaded to back off, to believe the unbelievable (such as "he has a good heart," even though he's obviously a gangster, or, "I rarely smoke any more," even though she looks high all the time and has probably gained twenty-five pounds from junk food).

Andrea is trapped by the "I owe" lie because she feels to blame for the possibility that her daughter was abused by Chuck.

This belief has tremendous power to keep family members stuck in the goo of exaggerated or hostile dependency cycles (see chapter 5). Like Andrea, stuck family members hold on to the memory of an event, episode, or era that is believed or known to have harmed a loved one. They feel responsible and carry the blame and shame for what happened, believing they can and should make up for or repair the damage. The result is an inability to set clear boundaries or hold limits. Andrea cannot expect to be treated fairly or kindly and tolerates her daughter's assaults on her character, finances, and generosity, as well as on herself. As a result, Cyndi gets the message that her pain takes priority and that her mother, and maybe the world, will arrange itself to soothe her. In addition, family members like Cyndi learn that others will overlook the destructive ways they engage in (lying, using, neglecting, acting out). Instead, the guilty "I owe" believer will cover up for, repair, and deny the effects of those behaviors on the person, themselves, and the family.

So, What's the Lie? Identifying the Distortion

Living in "I owe" includes believing that you can undo damage from the past or give a loved one new DNA or a new poker hand in the master game of life. The distortion locates responsibility for a loved one's wounds in events of the past, exempting that person from facing hurts in much the same way as substance abuse, mood swings, or self-harm may do. In turn, this deprives the problematic member of the family of necessary developmental struggles and internal work needed to mature or become independent. This lack of developmental struggling promotes weakness and perpetuates helplessness, relapse, and distress in the system.

Toward the end of this chapter strategies to step away from "I Owe" and the other lies are provided.

Next, let's take a look at:

"I CAN'T STAND HIS/HER DISCOMFORT"

Many family members feel taken over or panicked when learning of their loved one's distress, discomfort, or dangerous situation. When activated in this way, family members swoop in to rescue, protect, soothe, and smooth things over. If you believe the person you love lives at risk of getting hurt, overdosing, being a crime victim or similar, it's natural to be protective and easily activated; however, when based on an inability to tolerate the loved one's discomfort, this protectiveness will cost dearly. And, as with the searching behavior in "If only I can find . . . ," soothing a distressed loved one can feel good and distract you from your own discomfort—another perpetuating factor.

One cost of this lie involves the way in which swooping in at the first sign of discomfort perpetuates "the identified patient" setup. In this model, we have "healthy ones" who provide care and "sick ones" who need help. "Learned helplessness" describes how this occurs and its effects.[1] When we respond to the discomfort signal of our loved one with what may be unnecessary "first aid," we interrupt that person's essential development. Birds shoved out of the nest are likely quite uncomfortable in that moment. Yet, if momma birds didn't do this, birds would never fly.

Lastly, maintaining the rescuing position in "I can't stand her discomfort" can send a covert message received by your loved one as "I need you to need me." Many a young adult child with serious problems stays sick to serve as a repair project for a parent. This maintains the cycles of exaggerated or hostile dependency and can last for decades.

When we become able to withstand our loved one's discomfort, we contradict this covert message, instead saying, "I believe you have what you need to deal with this."

So, What's the Lie? Identifying the Distortion

The lie here, simply, is that the loved one's pain cannot be endured. The truth is you not only can but must learn to tolerate the discomfort experienced by struggling loved ones. Recovery only happens in the presence of discomfort—not unlike surgery. This underscores the importance of building a network of allies who will walk with you through doing things differently, increasing your ability to tolerate your loved one's discomfort and resist disabling rescuing.

Finally, we have one more relatively common lie:

"SHE'LL RELAPSE IF I . . ."

In this gripping and powerful story, a parent or spouse gives in to unreasonable demands, enters into unrealistic agreements, or continues serving and soothing their problematic loved one based on a relapse threat (expressed or imagined). You are led to believe you could either cause or prevent relapse. The threat of relapse could be in your mind or said directly by your loved one.

Bill is just beginning to trust Levi, who is three weeks out of rehab and living in a sober home. Levi has had a very poor record with cars: two DUIs and two serious crashes. Remarkably, he's been uninjured physically. They're in a familiar conversation, which ends sounding like this:

"Well, Dad, if you won't get me a car, I'm not sure I can get to meetings. And they say, 'meeting makers make it.'"

This goes through Bill like a sword. He feels so responsible!

That feeling of responsibility can be nearly overwhelming. Many parents in this position buy the car despite the evidence suggesting it will not be operated or maintained reliably or will be driven while inebriated. The responsibility feeling is driven by the distorted part of the belief in which you're responsible for a possible relapse. *If you're powerful enough to cause a relapse, why aren't you powerful enough to cause sobriety?* You haven't been able to strike them sober, nor have you managed to get them to take their medication, go to therapy, or get up in the morning. You're not that powerful. Knowing this proves you really can't make them relapse. There are probably dozens of thoughts or events that can prompt someone to relapse. What they've learned in recovery and how they deal with difficulty, manage anxiety, and use their coping toolkit will determine their relapse risk. Let the evidence of your inability to prevent previous relapses be proof that you can't cause the next one if it's going to occur.

Bill might say something like:

"Well, son, we both know there's a long list of reasons why you might relapse. I see you doing well working your program and I'm proud of you. Let's go to Target and get you some new sheets like we planned."

It's entirely possible, though certainly hopeful, that Levi might reply:

"Okay. Actually, Dad, I've been having pretty good luck getting rides so far."

INTERRUPTING THE LIES AND THEIR POWER

As explained previously, family system recovery involves changing beliefs. The Lies That Bind are among the most powerful. They hold family members in "classic" ways of responding that keep the cycles of dependency and relapse going. Freedom from the lies starts with putting the beliefs into words. Next, identify the distortion, the part that's inaccurate, by questioning the belief to find its distortions. When the belief can be shown to be a lie, refusing to be held in its grip becomes easier and eventually, quite natural.

Here are some questions to probe your beliefs. Consider them carefully. They'll guide you to identify the distortions and lies. Performing this exercise in and of itself creates a shift away from the identified patient setup (what's wrong with him?) as you pursue the more powerful question, what's true about me?

1. What evidence supports my belief?
2. What situations and feelings activate the belief and make me act upon it?
3. What are the advantages (benefits) of holding this belief and acting on it?
4. What's the cost or toll on me or the system of holding/acting on this belief?
5. What would my loved one say about my belief? Would the person agree?
6. What would I have to face if I admitted the parts of the belief that are distorted or untrue? How would that feel?

Beneath most distorted beliefs there is powerful evidence supporting it: life-threatening danger, essential missing elements, or trauma from the past. Our challenge involves accepting the evidence and adopting a more realistic and healthy approach to deal with it.

Let's do a practice run through these questions using Kathleen's story relayed at the beginning of this chapter. Her daughter, Jenny, has had several ER trips and been near death related to her alcohol abuse and anorexia. She's only sixteen, so Kathleen is often near panic and has been caught in "I'm keeping her alive" for several years.

Question 1: What evidence supports my belief? The belief is "I'm keeping her alive." For Kathleen, the evidence is powerful and compelling. She believes that she is keeping her daughter alive because Jenny has been near death more than once. One time, it was Kathleen who got help for Jenny. In addition, Jenny has a condition that is truly life threatening.

Question 2: What situations and feelings activate the belief and make me act upon it? Kathleen could easily talk about the situations that activate her:

Jenny drunk, Jenny looking thinner, Jenny talking about or restricting her food, Jenny going out with or talking about being with an older boy. After reflecting a bit, Kathleen could observe her most common activating feelings: anxiety, fear, and terror. This is certainly understandable. When in the grip of fear that Jenny is in danger or presently may be, Kathleen springs into rescue or protect mode.

Question 3: What are the advantages (benefits) of holding this belief and acting on it? Holding the belief that she's keeping her daughter alive provides Kathleen a feeling that she has some control and can help when Jenny's in danger. Acting on the belief, or simply planning ways to respond in the future, distracts Kathleen from her powerlessness. Remember, Jenny would say her mother cannot reliably keep her alive, thus proving Kathleen's powerlessness. Believing she's keeping her daughter alive relieves the awful powerlessness.

Question 4: What's the cost or toll on me or the system of holding/acting on this belief? "I'm keeping her alive" is an expensive belief and takes a significant toll: hours of anxious worry and monitoring and a corrosion of closeness with the loved one when snooping, supervising, lecturing, or pressuring. The loved one will often feel controlled, mistrusted, even shamed. One becomes trapped and misses out on what might be personally meaningful activities because they might interfere with remaining "on the case." Vacations get postponed, work opportunities turned down, exercise or other fun away from home is reduced or dropped. These all have adverse health effects and will cause other relationship difficulties, particularly with one's spouse or partner. "Stop worrying, Kathleen," her husband would say. "We have to learn to trust her a little." Kathleen might heed his advice when Jenny is active in treatment and doing better; however, when Jenny is declining or in trouble, Kathleen becomes taken over by her fear, and reflexively launches into protector mode.

The recovery method outlined in this book reconditions your reflexes away from the other-awareness necessary to maintain the IP setup and toward self-understanding and compassion.

Question 5: What would my loved one say about my belief? Would the person agree? This is a difficult question. I've asked hundreds of loved ones, typically when they are in treatment, what they think about their family members' distorted beliefs about them. If Kathleen were to discuss with Jenny her belief that she's keeping her daughter alive, Jenny would say, "Mom, you can't do that." And this would be patently true. As discussed in the detail about this lie, the at-risk members readily admit that others can't reliably keep them alive. Jenny would tell her mother to live her life as fully as she can: "My recovery is my responsibility," many like her say. She'd want nothing more than for her mother to be free of the trap of believing she's keeping her daughter alive.

Question 6: What would I have to face if I admitted the parts of the belief that are distorted or untrue? How would that feel? This is the most painful part of this questionnaire. If Kathleen admitted that she can't keep Jenny alive, she would have to face the fact that she might one day lose her to anorexia and/or an overdose. Life-threatening disordered eating combined with alcohol abuse is the most fatal behavioral health care condition by a factor of ten—that's truly disturbing to any parent or partner. How would that feel? Downright awful, no doubt. Rather than acknowledge this awful risk, family members are held hostage in the grip of "I'm keeping her alive." Ironically, the corrosion of closeness along with the reduction in quality of life for the family organized around keeping a member alive are far more destructive than facing the risk to the loved one.

> When you make your quality of life and serenity the top priority, problematic loved ones are much more likely to make a project out of their lives and their recovery.

The recovery process described in this book does not require abandoning loved ones or magically accepting or "letting go" of the fear they might die or leave you. Absolutely not. The goal involves detaching from the detail and the drama of their condition and their lives. When you make your quality of life and serenity the top priority, problematic loved ones are much more likely to make a project out of their lives and their recovery.

The rest of this book, particularly chapters 7 through 9, will show you how to do this. Hang in there and keep going.

Now let's take each lie, in turn, and talk about how to reduce its grip.

"I'm Keeping Her Alive"

As mentioned, this is the most disabling and powerful belief. The terror of losing a child or spouse overwhelms and strangles us. It's also true, as explained above, that it contains an essential distortion, the lie part: You can't reliably keep this person alive. The person knows it too and will tell you flat out: "You can't prevent me from . . ."

Operating on the impossible belief that you can or must do so keeps you stuck. We saw in the worksheet questions that the distortion you'd have to face means accepting that it's possible that you will lose this person to death, incarceration, or insanity. And as horrible as it sounds to admit that, we must face it to gain some separation from "I'm keeping her alive." Here's what we might say to ourselves, instead:

"If I were to lose her, that would be a tragedy from which I, our family, and our friends would never fully recover. It would be the worst event of my life. Yet, I know I can't reliably keep her alive. My job is to create the closest connection with her that I can without being taken over by this lie and the chaotic action I get involved in when I believe it."

"If Only I . . ."

This is another powerful story that holds people for years. Parents say things like: "We just want to get through this semester, get her out of high school, complete this medication trial, get through her brother's wedding," and so on. The list can be endless. The problem with this post-ponement method, although it makes total sense at the time, is that five or ten years can go by and you're identifying the next hurdle to jump or river to cross and nothing has changed. In fact, by then, things will probably be more stuck than ever.

For the regret version of "If only I . . . ," begin by admitting you can't change the past. Put into words why you made various choices. Some of these thoughts might sound like: "We had to move, the neighborhood was deteriorating," or "Yes, I married that person, I was in love and lonely." The goal is to move toward saying something like: "It's true, that happened. I made that choice. Now, what relationship (connection) can we have today?"

For the aspirational version of "If only I find . . . ," start by recognizing:

1. There isn't any one thing that's going to straighten things out or put your loved one on the right path. The evidence of that person's life and your efforts thus far proves this.

2. Many of the things you're searching for will only have use when your loved one seeks and finds them. While it's true you likely have located important and useful resources for your loved one, in a very unfair way it may also be true that your obtaining them has tainted your loved one's ability to embrace them. You may hear something like: "Well, you found me that therapist; I never really liked him." Or "You made me go to that outpatient program; it's stupid."

3. This one might be the most painful. Older teens and young adults reach a point in their development where they no longer expect their parents to understand them well enough to know what they really need. As a result, they cannot receive leads, suggestions, links, or referrals from you as they might from a peer or admired elder (counselor, teacher, coach, etc.). Probably in your own life, around age seventeen or eighteen, you knew it was up to you. That's not just culturally determined, it's a developmental norm. The challenge is to accept that even though your internet searches are skillful and your willingness to pay, drive them, and wait for them are good and useful, they just can't make use of these from you. This makes the argument to turn that searching, seeking, and escorting effort toward yourself: A vacation? A course of study? A massage series? A romantic partner (if you're single today)? That's where to redirect "If only I . . ." energy.

"I Owe"

The solution for "I owe" is similar to the regret version of "If only I." Begin by acknowledging the hurt your loved one reports from events of the past. If the person says it hurt, even if you don't agree it should hurt as much as represented, simply acknowledge the hurt.

This could sound like: "I know what happened hurt you," or "I am truly sorry for how much this hurt you." Then, continue with something like: "I've been trying to make up for it for many years. I can't change that _____ (fill in the blank: 'Dad left us,' 'I drank,' 'we moved and you lost your friends,' or whatever it was). I get that you are _____ (angry, resentful, not going to speak to him). I see now that I can't make up for it and I'm going to stop trying so I can be healthy."

This next part is critical, so do not skip it: "What I am available for is the closest and best relationship we can have. So, we said we would go to the _____ (park, baseball game, frozen yogurt shop). I'm looking forward to that."

In short, we do several things:

1. Acknowledge the person's pain.
2. Admit we've been trying to fix or make up for the past.
3. Declare we will no longer do so.
4. Offer connection and availability to be together and get closer.
5. Accept that the person may remain angry, hurt, or resentful. Don't try to change that. You can choose connection even if your loved one needs to hold on to the pain, resentment, frustration, or anger from the past.

"I Can't Stand His Discomfort"

You *can* stand his discomfort and need to learn how to do so. Recovery, like surgery, necessarily involves discomfort. By attempting to spare your loved one the uncertainty, anxiety, or pain associated with growing up or getting well, you are interfering with that person's recovery and development.

When your loved one is conditioned by your behavior to believe you can't stand seeing the loved one's discomfort, this person will be quick to report any such discomfort, may exaggerate it, and will deepen the unhealthy dependency between you. So, set the loved one and yourself free as follows:

1. Pause when you are made aware of the person's discomfort. Rather than swoop in and help or solve it, see how your loved one deals with it on their own.
2. Use the language: "I believe you have what you need to sort this out." You can follow this by asking: "What might you need from me?" You might be surprised; the person could say: "I just wanted you to know." Or the person might realize it is something that can be self-provided.
3. Don't be alone doing this. You'll be in some pain when you don't swoop in and soothe. Psychotherapy, Al-Anon meetings, or a parent/spouse support group are among the most helpful.

4. Develop a set of trusted allies who "get it." They're most readily located in Al-Anon meetings. Then call and make use of them: "My daughter just told me someone in the treatment center stole her lighter and she has no mascara. I'm dying to go to CVS and FedEx her those things." The Al-Anon member might respond by saying, "I'm glad you called. I know that feeling really well. Are you free for lunch?"

"He'll Relapse If I . . ."

This is our last lie. Many parents or partners have this one hanging over their heads. As explained earlier, you cannot make someone relapse by pursuing your own needs and health; however, the loved one might prefer that you believe that you can cause their relapse. Why might the person do this? So that you continue to give support, limit what you insist upon, maintain flimsy limits and boundaries, and provide resources or opportunities. The way out of this lie involves knowing there are dozens of reasons or rationales over which one can relapse. I have asked hundreds of clients in addiction treatment whether their loved ones can "make them" relapse. Virtually all say: "No. My recovery is up to me." They will also admit that they prefer others, like parents, believe they're responsible. When that's the case, they have more power to get what they want and to make their lives easier. Obviously, such a condition promotes exaggerated and prolonged dependency. Recognize your powerlessness either to make the loved one relapse or get healthy or sober. Freedom from the relapse responsibility lie will follow immediately.

KEY TAKEAWAYS

All the lies can be weakened by noticing the degree to which they are distorted—that is, identifying the lie portion. At the same time, give yourself a break; every one of these stories contains some truth. That's what makes them so compelling. The work to free yourself happens in your mind and with the help of your recovery allies: recognize what you believe, inventory its evidence, identify the distortion, and then embrace a more realistic way of thinking and the freedom it brings. ("I can't keep her alive, but I'll call 911 if I think she's suicidal.") Build a network of trustworthy allies such as other parents or partners who "get it." Engage an informed therapist, try group therapy, and investigate a handful of Al-Anon meetings. Most important: be kind to yourself. You came upon these beliefs honestly and have been held in their grip for understandable reasons. Now, it's time to set yourself (and your loved ones) free.

• 4 •

Intergenerational Insanity

The Impaired Coping Model

Shift your system toward wellness by interrupting the ways you learned to cope.

"*W*ait till you father gets home," was Mom's typical warning. It told us we'd be held to account, punished perhaps, and reminded all of us there was a source of ultimate authority to correct and guide us. Mom relied on Dad to straighten things out, establish order, and uphold the rules.

In the Rossi family, Dad coming home was a mixed bag. Mom, who spent her afternoons in a calico apron preparing elaborate dinners and desserts, learned over the years that "wait till your father gets home" might not be something she should rely on. For it had become true for quite some time that any of several versions of Anthony Sr. could show up, or sometimes he wouldn't show up at all.

By the time he was thirteen, Anthony Jr. had learned to listen attentively at his upstairs window for the sounds of his father's arrival. A. J. spent his afternoons on his bed, reading comics or doing homework with his ear near the screen. Based on the crunch or squeal of the tires on the gravel, the way the car and house doors closed, and the overall speed with which Anthony Sr. made it from the car to the house, Jr. could predict which version of "your father" he had been waiting for. Perhaps Dad would be jovial, bring unexpected presents, and kiss and hug everyone with proclamations of love. A day or two later, he might slam the car door, noisily open and close a few kitchen cabinets and the fridge, and then retreat to his den for the evening, from which loud rock music would fill the small frame house. Mrs. Rossi, Connie, knew to avoid her husband on those evenings. Or, worst of all, Anthony Sr. could show up closer to 10 p.m. than 6 p.m. and be in "Great Santini mode," as Anthony and his sister called it after seeing Robert Duvall in the famous film. On these nights there would be inspections and corrections: beds were stripped, knapsacks upended, kids lined up in the kitchen, inspected then reprimanded for infractions real or imagined. Report cards that already had been seen and signed were again reviewed, confessions were demanded ("Admit you let that neighbor kid Carlos feel you up!" he once screamed at Jr.'s younger sister, Carla, with his nose inches from hers). Connie barely contained her husband from hitting his daughter.

On these nights the bourbon and beer were always close by.

As you read through this vignette, notice the wounded family features: fear, control, anxiety, disorder, doubt (uncertainty about which Dad would arrive), despair, and denial.

EXAMINING THE DEAL

The Rossi family, like so many others, displays the classic features of an alcoholic family system, including in its ancestry. Connie's father was an alcoholic; Anthony Sr.'s father, August, brought the family from Calabria, Italy. He had left school after sixth grade. He ruled with an iron fist, worked eighteen hours a day, and died of a stroke at sixty-two. His wife, Carlotta, never learned much English. She cooked, cleaned, served, and soothed her husband and seven children. Anthony Sr. was the youngest. He believed he had to prove himself lest he be overlooked and irrelevant.

While some might characterize the Rossi family of today as "dysfunctional," as explained in chapter 1, it will be more accurate to describe them as wounded. Each is struggling to cope with life in their system, wounded by a legacy of control behavior, alcoholism, loss, displacement, disconnection, and disorder. Although Anthony Sr. knows something is very wrong, he is caught in his own trauma history with its associated powerlessness; he copes by drinking and then the alcohol takes over his mind and his body.

Many would say if Anthony Sr. would stop drinking, things would be fine. This is a reasonable assumption, since it seems much of the systemic distress can be attributed to Sr.'s unpredictability and rages, which occur only when he has been drinking. But, "fix him and we'll be fine" is a trap that holds many alcoholic systems stuck for decades and even generations.

In the recovery model outlined in this book, we work to understand, address, and shift the system, not just a single member. We start by putting into words the system's characteristics and rituals. Ask: "What's the deal we're in with each other?" rather than "How can we get Dad sober?" In the Rossi family, like all wounded families, each member plays a role or part in the system's functioning. These roles are taken on to help members cope with the pain of life in the system and the household environment. As the pain intensifies, the role structure becomes increasingly rigid and relied upon, and the patterns are repeated from one generation to the next.

In the Rossi family, Mom and children live in response to Dad's moods and behavior. Here are their common methods to cope and survive:

- Connie cooks, cleans, serves, soothes, smooths things over, prays, and hopes for better times.
- Jr. listens at his window, tries to figure out what's coming next, and pursues high levels of academic and sports achievement in the hopes of pleasing his father (based on the false belief this will calm things down).
- Carla seeks the attention of boys, focuses incessantly on her appearance, while planning her escape. When younger, that involved a knight in shining armor fantasy; today it's a (premature) search for Mr. Right.
- Anthony Sr. works sixty-plus hours a week and drinks to escape the drudgery of his days and the traumas of his past.

Think about how the roles show up in your family both past and present.

The traumas endured by one's ancestors are transmitted in the DNA through an intergenerational transmission process. Epigenetic research has shown that a person's way of responding to uncertainty or violence (including loud noises or threats) is determined to a large degree by the interruptions in safety and subsequent coping experienced by previous generations of biological ancestors.[1] In other words, if one's ancestors survived the Holocaust, slavery, the loss of a home or fortune, the dismantling of a culture or way of life, their descendants might respond to uncertainty or violence as though they themselves had experienced the ancestor's trauma. Relational trauma describes interruptions in safety, which takes place in the caregiving environment; these emotional injuries are commonly found in addictive and personality disorders.

EXAMINING THE SYSTEM ENVIRONMENT

When we take a closer look at the environment, or climate, in a family system with addiction or mental illness in its midst, we find a set of common characteristics, "the six Ds." These include: *disorder, disconnection, deprivation, danger, doubt,* and *denial.* Let's examine them in turn.

Disorder

Wounded family systems are disordered in several ways. First, the very nature of life in the system may be described as out of order: things are chaotic, violent, unpredictable, and scary. Members often don't know what's coming next and spend considerable energy both trying to predict it or prevent it. What a toll this takes! Consider Anthony Jr.'s listening at the window for the sounds of his father's arrival and for clues about which version of Dad would arrive: friendly, withdrawn, or violent and scary. Jr. used tremendous amounts of brain power in this task; what better use might he have put this mental energy to were he not trying to manage his fear in this way? Disorder in the family system environment takes members out of themselves by promoting a fight/flight response that shuts down thinking, corrodes closeness, and leaves members in a chronic state of being on edge or walking on eggshells.

Disorder also captures the way in which the developmental process in wounded families can become out of order, or what I call "out of phase." This can be seen in what is best described as "parentification" of children.[2] When this type of disorder is present, the boundaries between parent and child, or some of the children, become blurred. Children are called upon to play parental roles or to soothe or protect a parent.

Gap-toothed with a mop of frizzy curls, Tanya is five years old. She takes great pride in caring for Shawn, who'll be two in a few months.

Family members say, "Look at Tanya with her little brother. She's so great, she changes diapers and does everything." Caring for Shawn makes Tanya feel grown up. She's had to get good at it. In the afternoons, shortly after coming home from kindergarten at lunchtime, Mom takes pills and drinks wine before her "nap time," passing out in front of the TV until just before Dad comes home around 5:30. Tanya remembers how angry he became when he came home to find Mommy asleep, the baby wet, and Tanya playing on Mom's cell phone. She has learned to care for Shawn and wake Mommy up before *Dr. Phil* ends at 4:30, well before Dad arrives. In a classic form of out-of-phase development, Tanya has become a "little Mommy" as her identity warps into that of the parentified child. As she ages, without help, her caregiving will become compulsive; her future as a fixer (described below) is virtually assured.

Out-of-phase development occurs when one of the children becomes a confidant for one or both parents. This is particularly damaging when one parent confides to the child about problems with the other parent. Unfortunately, this is all too common. When the child hears things like "I don't think Mommy loves me anymore," or "When you grow up make sure you don't marry someone like your father," two things happen: First, all kids between ages eight and twelve assume that whatever's wrong in the family is likely their own fault. This is just how kids are wired. And, when a kid takes the blame for the adults' problems, he or she will either try to fix things by being extra good, or perfect— they'll do anything not to makes things worse. Or this child might sink into despair or illness, thereby providing the parents a new problem to distract them from their marital woes. In either scenario, children cut themselves off from awareness of their own needs, rejecting natural childhood pastimes and interests to avoid adding to the parents' burden.

To manage the burden of the secrets they carry, these confidant kids will broker deals to smooth things between their parents. In turn, they get tangled up in adult concerns and emotional situations they don't fully understand; yet, they have to act as if they have things under control. This produces a kid with no clear sense of self, having adopted an identity as peacemaker or broker—another future fixer and disconnected system member.

The despairing/sick kids are engulfed by blame and self-loathing. They may get into fights, cut or disrupt school, shoplift, harm themselves (cutting, burning), or isolate themselves and withdraw from academic, social, and family life. They develop ever-worsening problems the parents may work to solve or deny and overlook. Often the despairing kids' problems become the focus of the family, distracting the parents from their own difficulties. Untreated, the despairing kids develop depression/anxiety disorders and a higher risk for suicide than others. In their early teens, they will find relief in marijuana and alcohol, thereby increasing their risk of chemical dependency.

Lastly, kids who respond by concealing their needs become the family's actors and entertainers (a form of "the distractor" as described later in this chapter), attempting to get their emotional and physical needs met through elaborate cover-ups, concealments, and repackaging or sanitizing their requests. "Dad, I think Sis is really thirsty; she might even be dehydrated. We should stop and get her some water." This, because he's secretly hoping the stop will include an opportunity for him to get a soda. His deeper belief is either that to ask for a soda for himself will bring on a scolding or shaming or that it's best to appear to have no needs of his own.

Of course, it's impossible for a kid to have no needs. The long-term effects of living as though one has none include disconnection from self and the development of a false identity. As these youngsters repeat and refine their "no needs" behaviors, they fade into the background because they're assumed to be fine. Theirs becomes an empty and lonely future, stuck in the impossible vortex between having needs that must be concealed and the ever-worsening experience of feeling invisible.

Disconnection

> Members of wounded family systems experience disconnection from each other along with a form of disconnection that takes place internally, within oneself.

Members of wounded family systems experience disconnection from each other along with a form of disconnection that takes place internally, within oneself.

Members disconnect from each other as the result of unresolved arguments, irreconcilable disputes, feuds and estrangements, abandonments, or other forms of leaving. Here's a common example: As Theresa is telling her daughter her plan about Thanksgiving, nine-year-old Sophie pushes her glasses up her nose, looks square into her mother's face: "But, Uncle Tony and Uncle Steve can't be in the same room with each other," she says authoritatively. "The lights will go out."

"Where on earth did you hear that?" Mother squeaks. But, she knows all too well one or both of her brothers say that thing about the lights. She realizes she herself never knew what that meant (except that it sounded violent). Now it's being parroted by her baby daughter.

Sometimes a situation like the one with Steve and Tony has gone on for so long no one recalls what originally drove them apart. Their mother has said, "Something about a girl Tony took to the prom that maybe Steve wanted to take, I don't really know." It can even be true that Steve or Tony doesn't really know either; however, the hate, disdain, and disconnection live on for decades.

Another form of disconnection involves leaving. In this case, a family member moves away from the family, often at a relatively young age. See the description of the "escapee" later in this chapter. In this form of disconnection, a member plans early in life to get out and get away, goes far away, refuses invitations to return, makes excuses for missing holidays, and becomes a foreigner to the family.

The other form of disconnection, the internal kind, involves separation from the self and one's fundamental goodness. As wounded family members begin the work outlined here, they discover they have difficulty knowing their own needs—they've been so long attuned to the needs of others. When asked about their emotions and feelings, they'll often answer with "Well, she . . ." or "When he . . ." They are conditioned to link their emotional understanding of themselves to the behavior or the thinking of others.

"What's it like when your daughter doesn't return your calls or texts and you see it's after midnight?" The therapist asks to probe the mother's emotional experience. The mother who is disconnected from herself will answer with something like:

"Well, I know she tries to take good care of herself and probably would call if she was in serious trouble."

"Yes, but what goes on inside you?" the therapist gently pushes a bit further.

"Well, if she has her phone, I know it might be turned off or if she's somewhere it's too loud for her to hear it ring, like a nightclub or a party or something like that." As becomes all too common, this mother can't identify her own emotional experience; she can't think about what goes on inside her and she has little or no language for it. Her fixer training has taught her to focus on the behavior, the likes/dislikes, the needs, and what she believes is going on in the mind of someone else (in this case her troubled daughter).

The recovery goal will be to help a mother in this position to say something like:

"I get all churned up inside, sweaty, panicky, and I can't stop wondering where she is and whether she's safe. It's awful."

As described in later chapters, developing the ability talk about one's self in this way, rather than focus on the troubled "other," begins the personal process of recovery.

As members of wounded family systems pursue recovery, starting with themselves, they frequently discover a belief, developed as children, that they are at fault, or are defective in some way. This can be thought of as a way of disconnection from one's sense of fundamental goodness—a sense with which virtually all of us are born. The effects include high anxiety, self-doubt, and difficulty making decisions.

As the Stress-Induced Impaired Coping (SIIC) model reveals later in this chapter, shame lives at the core of a family's woundedness; and that shame is most commonly expressed as a belief about being defective, broken, or "off" in some dreadful and irreparable way that must be kept hidden.

The next D word:

Deprivation

In many wounded families there occurs a shortage of the emotional nutrients necessary for healthy human development—the things that feed us to be emotionally healthy and balanced. When members from such systems are asked what they wish there had been more of growing up, here are the most common answers:

- time together
- time with Dad
- laughter
- guidance

- communication
- consistency
- fairness
- "I wish I was valued for what I was good at, not what they wanted me to be"
- clarity or consistency about the rules
- hugs
- safety
- freedom to express myself
- closeness

Given these responses gathered from several thousand family members in sessions and workshops, it's easy to see how the conditions essential for healthy emotional growth are in too short supply. Family members will figure out a way to cope with that shortage. As the SIIC model will explain, that coping takes place in a way that typically produces more loss or illness.

It's also true that life in wounded family systems is dangerous.

Danger

In a family with alcoholism or addiction in its midst, or with high levels of anxiety or controlling behavior, more frequent episodes of domestic violence, sexual abuse, and expressed rage occur than in the general population. In response, family members walk on eggshells, believing that doing so will avoid provoking an episode. Unfortunately, walking on eggshells doesn't create safety over time. One loses a sense of physical safety, and sexual boundaries are too often crossed.

Sexual boundary crossing includes:

- Comments made about a developing person's body ("You're gonna break a lot of hearts with a body like that.")
- Criticizing the expression of emotion in a sexual way ("Only fairies cry.")
- Leering or spying on a child's private body. This could take place around the bathroom, when getting dressed, or wearing night-clothes or bathing suits

- Sexualized touching including pinching, rubbing, pulling clothing down, examining developing sexual characteristics such as breasts or body hair
- Criminal sexual behavior including fondling, penetration, and rape

Another form of danger, perhaps the one most commonly found, involves the danger of being humiliated, usually by being exposed as inadequate or wrong. These include receiving messages in the family that one isn't athletic enough, smart enough, fast enough, tall enough, white/black/Latino/Asian enough, motivated enough, good-looking enough, well-groomed enough. The list is long. The humiliation can also take the form of being revealed as misunderstanding the situation, unable to read cues (labeled "clueless"), or accused of being dumb.

These experiences of boundary crossing or humiliation have a toxic effect on development, crush self-esteem, and produce a sense of self as defective or broken. By teenage years, a person plagued by such beliefs will find ways to ward them off. Alcohol, marijuana, excessive gaming, high-risk sexual behavior, self-harm, or disordered eating are the most commonly employed. Obsessing about the needs of others who appear to be in even greater distress might be another way of coping. More about this in the coping section later in this chapter.

Doubt

The word "doubt" makes the D list to describe how wounded families do a poor job of managing uncertainty or the unexpected, instead engaging in behaviors that increase stress levels. Under such conditions, impulsive decision-making occurs with little regard for the effect on family members. These decisions are arbitrary, often handed down as orders, thereby masking the way in which they're poorly thought through.

"Grandma broke her hip, so we can't go to her house for Thanksgiving," Dad announced at Sunday dinner. "So, we're bringing in Chinese and watching *Rocky*."

"What!" shrieked fifteen-year-old Andrew. "Can't I go with Jason's family to Tahoe?"

"Why don't we go to the family Thanksgiving our church is having?" said thirteen-year-old Jessica.

"It's a holiday. We need to be together." Dad's standing up now. "End of discussion."

Growing up under such conditions leaves one vulnerable to being indecisive or impulsive when facing uncertainty. High anxiety when facing decisions and avoidance of problem solving are common results. Blotting out one's awareness of a problem or responding impulsively or dramatically to the unexpected are additional likely effects.

Our last D, as they say, "is not a river in Africa."

Denial

Wounded family systems operate in their classic ways for decades. The levels of disorder, disconnection, and danger, the shortage of emotional goodies as well as the effects of impulsive decision-making, go unexamined and unquestioned. It is generally not possible for members even to wonder about or notice what's going on, let alone speak about it. This creates a psychological form of denial in which these things can't be considered. They don't come to mind. The risk of being humiliated and setting off a violent confrontation, sparking a new feud, estrangement, or loss of a member (who leaves), seems unbearable to cause. Instead, members soldier on across the years, decades, and generations, denying the truth and transmitting this denial-based impaired coping to the next generation.

STRESS-INDUCED IMPAIRED COPING: THE MODEL

Human beings are great at coping and adapting even to the most adverse or stressful conditions. We survive in ghettoes, outer space, the Arctic, or at sea. We sustain ourselves in deserts, frozen climes, packed cities. We survive diseases, famines, droughts, and wars. People have developed profound ways of coping with extreme conditions even when threatened with the risk of danger, pain, and death.

In family systems with addiction or mental illness in their midst or in their ancestry, members cope with the fear, uncertainty, and pain by employing one of several methods: escaping, fixing, blaming, or distracting. Each of these can be thought of as a role a member plays, or becomes, usually for quite a long time in the family life cycle. Let's look at each one in turn.

Escaping

Escaping through various means represents the most common coping method. Members escape in one of two ways: leaving or numbing themselves.

Leaving. As discussed in the disconnection section above, this escapee physically leaves the family, often when relatively young. It is common for this teen to leave behind a sibling with emotional or behavioral problems who has commanded high levels of attention and resources for years. This escapee has likely been thought of as "fine," when another child was "the problem." Semesters abroad turn into five- or ten-year relocations, international travel becomes a regular feature of everyday life, moving cross-country with a new life partner or choosing a college based on it being as far away as possible are a few examples.

Alternatively, it is possible for family members to leave psychologically or emotionally. They may withdraw into their room, their study, or their career. This can take the form of the super-busy family member who never slows down or rarely spends time at home. A person like this who is high achieving may be playing the role of distractor (described on the next pages).

Numbing Out. The other method of escaping involves numbing oneself. Family members may numb themselves with:

- alcohol and other drugs, including prescription drugs
- food and food-related compulsive behaviors, including restricting food intake, bingeing/purging, or obsessive calorie counting and measuring
- high-risk or high-frequency sexual activity, including use of pornography, compulsive masturbation, or volatile/turbulent serial relationships
- self-harm including cutting or burning
- suicidal obsessing or para-suicidal activity
- video gaming or other overuse of electronics including social media

Main effects of escaping. Escapees create problems to which other members react. Family members try to get through to them and fix them. Methods range from kicking them out to searching for them in order to bring them back (especially if they left when young). In addition, punishing, blaming, berating, bribing, or bargaining are common responses to the escapee's various forms of leaving. Escapees report feeling blamed, bothered, under a microscope, afraid, and ashamed. Numbing oneself makes it possible to get rid of or deny these feelings. Leaving permits an escapee to avoid contact with the environmental turmoil in the system (six Ds), though loneliness and isolation frequently plague them.

Outcomes. Untreated escaping behaviors result in serious conditions threatening the quality and length of life of an escapee. Addicts and those with compulsions or disabling obsessions chase their substances, behaviors, or ideas "to the gates of insanity or death," as described in the *Alcoholics Anonymous* textbook.[3] Escapees worsen over time, sometimes quite rapidly, and develop serious interpersonal and health problems. Without help, escapees lose health, hope, sanity, freedom, and self-respect.

Fixing

Most people reading this book will have played some version of the fixer role. These are the directors, brokers, and martyrs who dedicate themselves to serving, soothing, smoothing, or otherwise trying to straighten out another family member, or members, or even the system itself. Fixers are taken over by their beliefs about the needs of others. Over time, fixers become unaware of their own needs. (See disconnection section on page 52.) For most fixers this pattern began in early childhood when relied upon to provide caregiving or to keep secrets in the context of a blurry boundary with a parent or caregiver. Fixers are rewarded and reinforced for their efforts to serve or care for others; people want more and sometimes things get fixed. Compulsive fixing leads to loss of self-awareness, self-knowledge, and self-esteem.

Fixers come in three forms: directors, brokers, or martyrs.

Directors tell everyone how to conduct themselves and hold high expectations for conformity. When others don't cooperate, corrections, punishment, verbal violence, or other interventions follow. Directors need to be in charge. They genuinely believe they know what's right, what's best for others, and how to proceed. Others respond by conforming or defying; either one keeps the directing effort going.

Brokers make deals believing they can keep everyone "happy" by figuring out what others need and trying to provide or talk them into accepting a substitute. Brokers manage complex family situations, especially involving feuds, estrangements, or long-standing hurts. A favorite example is the broker who tries to make Thanksgiving work for everyone in the extended family, given that her two brothers have been feuding for more than a decade. She arranges to take certain foods to one brother's home in the morning, then sneaks out at midday to go the other brother's house with a different set of offerings. All the while, she pretends to be unaffected by the brothers' war with each other, a war the origins of which the two barely recall and may not agree upon. (See Steve and Tony's story earlier on page 53.)

Martyrs rely on infinite giving (cooking, cleaning, shopping, helping) to soothe others and themselves. They work themselves to the bone, expecting their sacrifices to be rewarded by better behavior from their problematic loved ones. Of course, this rarely works, and the martyrs are routinely disappointed, let down, overlooked, taken for granted, and expected to do even more. Martyrs cope with the pain of life in the family through incessant activity and sacrifice.

Main effects of fixing. Emotionally, fixers report they often feel anxious, used, drained, rejected, and depressed. Others respond by expecting more, relying on the fixing, or mocking the fixer and her methods (men can be fixers, too, of course). Fixers avoid the pain of life in the wounded family system by giving directions, making complex deals and arrangements, or shouldering impossible and never-ending burdens.

Outcomes. The future for the chronic fixer is not bright. Invariably, fixers fail to straighten others out. Fixers get worse as their project family members get worse. Fixers end up on a roller coaster, feeling increasingly out of control, overwhelmed, taken over, blamed, at fault, and like a failure. As the nest empties and the failure of the fixer's methods becomes more obvious, fixers turn to alcohol or other tranquilizers; develop depression, insomnia, and anxiety conditions; fail to care for themselves; and, ultimately, die younger than they should.

Blaming

Blamers can either be finger pointers or scapegoats.

Finger pointers blame one member or a situation as the problem; when that person or situation remains problematic, the blamer holds to their view. If the situation resolves, the blamer typically finds another target. This becomes a rigid and recurring theme in the blamer's language and style of interaction in the family. Sarcasm may be a common feature as the finger pointer pollutes the family environment with their caustic, cutting criticism and blame. "Oh, let me guess, you're going out with what's his name again. Don't forget to get drunk and wake us up at 3 a.m."

The other version of blame-based impaired coping involves taking on the role of *scapegoat*—the one who is blamed. You might wonder how this is an effective coping strategy. By being the one always in trouble the scapegoat controls the focus in the family and the attention they receive. They resolve their anxiety by knowing that others will respond to them in blaming, correcting, and shaming ways. Scapegoats describe the advantages to playing their role: in addition to the extra and predictable form of attention they obtain, others reduce their expectations of them, believing the scapegoat will get it wrong or mess it up.

"In the end they didn't even ask me to take out the garbage," a twenty-year-old who had been in trouble since his early teens reported. "They figured I'd screw that up, too."

Main effects of blaming. Blamers and blamed ones feel powerless, misunderstood, lonely, and desperate. Others respond by ignoring them or punishing them. Finger pointers may be mocked behind their backs, feared, despised, or all the above. They feel great pressure to get others to understand and join them in solving the problem as they see it. This leads to chronic feelings of powerlessness and anger. Blamed ones (scapegoats) feel anxious, invisible or under a microscope, powerless, out of control, ignored, or stuck on a treadmill. They may be held accountable for their problematic behavior, ridiculed, or told they'll be in the wrong again, soon. As the family's confidence and trust in them wanes, they lose the opportunity to excel or grow in healthy ways.

Outcomes. As with the other roles described so far, blamers are looking at a painful, unrewarding, and loss-filled future. Blamers become rageful and lose the affection and respect of other family members as they insist on their view and pressure others to engage in their proposed solutions. They become marginalized and isolated, often seeing their adult children only a few hours per year. Depression, chronic stress conditions, loneliness, and substance abuse follow.

Scapegoats resort to increasingly criminal behaviors. What might have led to a reprimand in teenage life can become a prison sentence for a young adult or grown person. Scapegoats turn to alcohol and other tranquilizers to ease the pain of being marginalized and outside of healthy groups. Untreated, depression, isolation, increased suicide risk, incarceration, and early death are among their unsavory fates.

Distracting

Distractors command attention, control resources, and are sources of pride. They are relied upon as the proof the family is okay. These are the high achievers, superstars, super-providers, and entertainers of the family.

Superstars get everything right, providing the most compelling proof the family is "fine." They get superior grades; win gold ribbons, scholarships, and other awards; attain athletic heights; or ascend organizational ranks in startlingly swift fashion. This generally begins in childhood and peaks in late teens or early adulthood. The superstar expects to be admired and receives special privileges and exceptions.

Super-providers bring in money and command financial and material resources. They may run the family business, hold professional positions with significant rank or acclaim, or use other methods (including crime) to produce financial gain. They expect to be revered, respected, and listened to. Importantly, they also expect to be exempt from the emotional life of the family, frequently claiming they are too busy to be involved in the worry, concern, pain, or uncertainty of other family members. One high-powered father summed it up in response to his son's complaint: "Emotionally unavailable!" father barked. "What do you mean I'm emotionally unavailable? If it wasn't for me, you wouldn't have the BMW you drove to get the DUI in the first place."

Lastly, the *entertainers* are the Robin Williamses of the family who keep everyone laughing and amused. They will go to great lengths to provide comic relief. They crave and receive attention while providing an effective distraction when things become awkward, uncomfortable, uncertain, or violent. The entertainer cracks jokes, dresses in funny outfits, spits food, acts the fool, or recites Shakespeare. They can seem desperate and are often unable to be serious when that's needed.

Main effects of distracting. Distractors are fragile and frequently immature or underdeveloped in emotional areas. Yet they are frequently seen as the family heroes. While they make it possible for members to believe everything is okay, distractors obsess over their achievements and are often quite anxious and insecure beneath the surface. They may have poor judgment about when to entertain and are unable to read social cues or determine what's appropriate for emotional situations. They're often seen as out of sync. Others respond by wanting more: more achievement, more money and things, more laughs. In turn, distractors feel valued and relied upon, though they can't consider what else others might need from them (such as to slow down or be emotionally present).

Outcomes. Most distractors burn out in their roles. A high school senior was head cheerleader, dating the captain of the football team, president of the math club, and hosting Sunday teas for exchange students. On Saturdays she brought sandwiches to the homeless shelter. She visualized obtaining a scholarship to Brown University or a similar Ivy League school. When she achieved a milestone, was elected to a new office, or enlisted others to her causes, she moved on to the next thing, always needing more. If she goes to Brown, she will repeat the pattern: incessant, insatiable achievement. Some would say, "What's wrong with high achievement? I want that daughter." Be cautious. When this level of achievement occurs in the context of the distractor role in a wounded family system, young women like these are at very high risk of disordered eating. Similarly, the relentlessly driven super-provider burns out, increases alcohol or other drug use, takes up a secret sex life, or crashes hard. The entertainers end up invisible with no one knowing the real person beneath and little ability to know themselves. Depression, isolation, substance abuse, and suicide risk mount for all forms of distracting.

ROLES SUMMARY

The roles described all serve a common purpose: to make the pain of life in the wounded family system environment tolerable and to stabilize the system by creating a balance or homeostasis that supports the system's ongoing functioning. At the same time, playing one's role is costly and takes a significant toll—increased losses and probable premature death.

All family members experience *Stress-Induced Impaired Coping* to varying degrees. It comprises the six Ds and the coping roles.

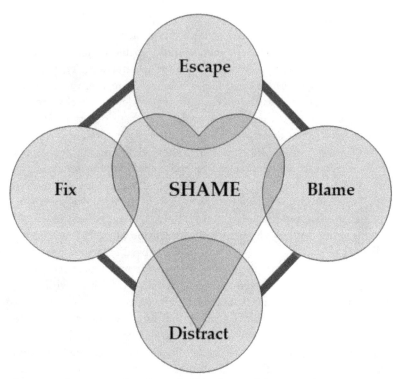

Figure 1. The Stress-Induced Impaired Coping Model

Consider your family of origin and the family you've created in modern times, notice which roles members take on or are pulled toward. The model isn't pure. No one takes on an exact replica of the roles as described here; however, it's likely that in a given wounded system some form of each role will be found. Keep in mind, members may trade roles, switching from one to another over the years. A one-time escapee who used marijuana and isolation might straighten up and become a fixer. Superstars crash and become escapees, turning to alcohol and other drugs to cope with the sense of failure. Frustrated fixers escape through drug use or shopping. Distractors burn out and turn to blaming an injury, the market, or corrupt business partners. In addition, a person's coping style can combine elements of more than one role, creating a hybrid form.

So, who has the best deal: escapees, fixers, blamers, or distractors? Well, as you've already figured out, there isn't a superior position. Everyone is coping as best they can, generally unaware of the problems that their impaired coping causes.

> Everyone is coping as best they can, generally unaware of the problems their impaired coping causes.

Notice the stability of the role structure in the diagram. Escapees, fixers, distractors, and blamers come together to form a powerful structure joined by biological and ancestral ties and held together by the power of the Lies That Bind (explained in chapter 3). The four roles bond to one another as shown, providing a stabilizing, counterbalancing force as the system spins through time and space. This setup, or constellation, maintains itself for generations, perpetuating the cycles of loss and illness.

As the diagram shows, the system rotates around a core, or center, at which lies the truth about the system. This includes the story history, the losses and traumas, and the painful features of the family and its ancestors believed to be too terrible to face. Members spin round and round across the generations, unable to examine the system or work together to change its harmful elements. The deeper, more painful, truth about "us" cannot be spoken. In turn, certain members end up expressing this pain through their destructive behaviors and mental illness.

The heart in the center of the model represents this painful and unspeakable truth. It lives at the core of wounded families and can best be described as shame. This shame lurks as an underlying fear that we are defective in some way that must be kept hidden. Secrets, lies, cover-ups, rewritten histories, and covert messages are manifestations of this shame. They are accompanied by rigidity, control, and high levels of environmental anxiety expressed by the six Ds described in chapter 1: disorder, disconnection, deprivation, danger, doubt, and denial.

See chapter 8 for a set of discovery questions to guide you toward a better understanding of Stress-Induced Impaired Coping including the six Ds and the impaired coping roles found in your family of origin and family of today.

In the next chapter we will explore enabling and look at how various forms of dependency can be thought about and worked through.

Deepening Our Understanding of the Family Deal

Early Influences, Failed Methods, Enabling, and Dependency

Abandon destructive enabling to give necessary and constructive help freely.

$\mathcal{A}$s explained in earlier chapters, we learned how to respond, relate, manage, interpret and express emotion, and cope with stress or uncertainty in our families of origin (FOO) and other early caregiving environments such as preschool and holiday gatherings. Our way of making sense of the world, our emotional intelligence, is based largely on what has been demonstrated for us. These experiences combine with our genetically determined style, our predispositions, and inform how we participate in the family deal. To examine the system, we look at our place in it, the ways members respond to one another and the problematic loved ones, and how each fits into the system. A similar examination is necessary for us, too. The goal is to be able to put into words the truth about your system and how you operate within it. Consider both the family in which you grew up as well as your family of today.

By engaging in such an examination, you'll begin to step out of the family chaos and move off the roller coaster on which so many have felt trapped. By distinguishing between enabling and necessary helping, you'll get clearer about when to help and when to back off.

EXAMINING THE FAMILY DEAL

This chapter will help you better understand the nature of dependency in relationships with your loved ones. Open your thinking to the concepts being introduced and the questions posed. Take these up as they relate to the family in which you grew up (family of origin) and, separately, your family of today. You will likely encounter many parallels or similarities—these themes repeat across the generations.

How Were Key Decisions Made?

This is a question about the nature of authority in the system. The most common answers are "Mom and Dad decided" or, simply, "Dad." In other families, "Mom decided but Dad announced it (so it looked like it was his idea)." Another response, "Seemed like nothing ever got decided." When there's a covert deal such as "Dad announced what was really Mom's plan," or a chaotic unpredictable method ("Seemed like nothing ever got decided") members are conditioned to accept covert operations as the norm or expect to be left to solve the problem themselves.

Deepening the inquiry, ask: How do I participate in the decision-making (authority) processes in my family today? How do others respond to my preferences, my needs, my authority? Is there an unspoken or covert authority structure existing outside the bounds of how decisions appear to get made (perhaps through favoritism or the overvaluing of one member's views)?

How Were Emotions Expressed?

Throughout our lives and our days, we see others when they're angry, anxious, sad, lonely, uncertain, or afraid. Children pay keen attention to how people respond to emotions expressed by the child and by others. In many families, suppressing emotion and minimizing its expression are mandatory: "Hey, knock it off; you're okay," might be the refrain in response to a child starting to cry. Along these lines, comments may be made about outsiders and their emotionality: "Aunt Peggy just has no filter; she's always worn her feelings on her sleeve." In another version, certain emotions are allowed, typically anger and "disappointment" (which really isn't an emotion, it's a judgment), while others are shameful to display, such as uncertainty, anxiety, or fear. "What's wrong with you?" might be the response. Lastly, and most commonly, certain emotions are permitted to be expressed by certain people: Dad yells in anger, Mom cries in frustration, Sister quakes in fear and uncertainty, Brother mopes and appears sad and lonely. Members learn to stifle their "unacceptable" emotions while internalizing a belief that certain emotions are shameful: Mom swallows her anger and blames herself, Dad hides uncertainty or anxiety (helped by alcohol perhaps), Sister suppresses confidence, and Brother restricts himself to depressive states.

As explained in the previous chapter, shame lies at the core of family system pain, exerting tremendous control over members' actions and thoughts. When an emotion is labeled as shameful, its expression will be avoided; however, doing so will, over time, be at the cost of sobriety, health, connection, interpersonal relationships, and self-esteem.

How Were Love and Affection Demonstrated?

Many say hugs and kisses were few and far between in their families of origin. "I Love You" was rarely, if ever, heard. Alternatively, many experienced high levels of emotional expression with syrupy displays of physical affection. "I Love You" statements abounded, often accompanied by demands for blind loyalty: "If you really loved me you would _____" (agree with me, keep my secret, stay home with me, etc.). The message received in each case was as follows: When expressions of love and affection (physical or verbal) were absent, one learned that to desire closeness or express affection is wrong and shameful. Excessive expressions of love left family members numb and unable to register their meaning. In these families, the loving statements or behaviors often didn't match the circumstances or conditions; this produced confusion and bewilderment. Love seemed to revolve around power, loyalty, or favoritism.

Lastly, many say that money was used to express love. In these cases, one was expected to be loyal, keep secrets, behave in a certain way, or avoid showing emotion or else lose the goodwill of the one with the purse strings.

How Were Crises Managed?

Consider how the family responded to crises such as a child suspended or expelled from school, a medical emergency or serious illness, car accident, loss of job or income, an assault, or other trauma. A decision-making process took place and others reacted. In some families, crises were managed thoughtfully, carefully, and in a way that matched the level of crisis. In wounded systems, there was either an overreaction that increased the level of distress, or an underreaction that minimized or overlooked the problem.

The overreactions added to the sense of danger, activated traumatic responses, and made it difficult to know how severe a problematic situation might really have been: Susie got suspended for cigarette smoking in the high school parking lot. Dad flipped out, threw chairs, blamed Mom and smashed Susie's cell phone, grounding her for a month. Susie ran to her room, slammed the door and broke her bathroom mirror, threatened to cut herself with the mirror shards, and run away. Mom spent the next two hours outside Susie's locked door pleading with her to calm down after Dad went to the bar. Younger brother stayed on his headphones in his room, playing a multiplayer video game.

This is the overreaction example. Consider what learning or conditioning each member is experiencing. What might a member of the family predict about how future difficulties will be handled. One assumption would be the kids and Mom would do everything they could to avoid upsetting Dad. This will require cover-ups, a corrosion of the parents' ability to partner around child rearing, and condition everyone to expect even small crises or life's curveballs to turn into violent overreactions involving threats, shaming, self-harm, and alcohol.

The underreactions left members shell-shocked and doubting themselves. A sense of learned helplessness likely followed accompanied by thoughts such as, "No one ever does anything." This produces children who must rely on childhood methods to solve complex problems. This produces adults with low self-esteem, difficulty partnering (at work or at home), high anxiety, procrastination, and apathy.

What Were You Valued and Praised For?

We learned what mattered about ourselves from the way people in our families of origin responded to us and treated us. We drew conclusions about what was good, important, and valuable. Through this early conditioning, we took on powerful beliefs about ourselves, our strengths and weaknesses, our abilities, and what qualities to display (and what aspects of ourselves we should hide). Encouraging messages came in the form of direct praise ("You're much prettier with your hair pulled back like that" or "Now that's a report card we should frame"), or nonverbal cues like smiles, nods, or winks. Similarly, discouraging messages could be overt ("I don't know why you want to go out looking like that") or indirect ("You wonder how that Jimmy kid gets so much playing time? Maybe it's because he can hit") or through more subtle, nonverbal communications like a look over the top of the eyeglasses, a sigh (of disgust), or members exchanging glances of disapproval with one another.

Too often, we were valued or praised for what others wanted us to be rather than what mattered most to us. Sports performance, grades, appearance and grooming, following directions or upholding family rules are among the most common responses to this question. While these are certainly important, and many tried to achieve in these ways, members of chaotic, disorganized, dangerous, or unpredictable environments wished for more attention, stability, looking out for each other, direction, guidance, or simply spending time together. Recall the list under "Deprivation" in "more of" from chapter 4.

Surprisingly, many adults who grew up in wounded family systems say they received no praise. In that situation, most people will make up a story for themselves about what's important or act out in ways to get noticed and at least receive some negative attention.

As you consider this question, ask what you value and praise in the others in your family of today. How well does what you praise them for match what they genuinely value for themselves? Do you let them know?

The next three questions begin a deeper inquiry into the family system itself. A common form of system pressure is identified, followed by a look at how that pressure caused problems and the ways in which members coped.

What Image Was the Family Expected to Portray?

In many, but not all, families the pressure was keen to maintain a certain appearance to outsiders and the community. Though parents rarely sat the kids down and explained this or spelled it out, rituals, comments, and ways of behaving demonstrated the importance of upholding a specific image of the family. This was often carried forward for generations or as part of a conscious attempt to appear different than the previous generation, which may have been too religious, too atheistic, too sloppy, too poor, or on the wrong side of the tracks. Again, verbal and nonverbal reinforcement for behaving in ways to uphold the image were provided.

Disparaging gestures or critical comments about other families who had the wrong appearance served to reinforce the importance of upholding the desired image.

Members of wounded families offer these as common images they were expected to uphold:

- We're good Catholics (or good Christians, Muslims, Jews, etc.).
- We have it together, perfect.
- We're smart, well educated.
- We're loving, charitable, and generous.
- We're antiestablishment or nonconforming.
- We're neat, tidy, good homeowners.
- We have money and status.

Some say there was no pressure to appear a certain way; however, consider the pressure upholding these might put upon the members of the family, especially the children. People say, "What's wrong with wanting to appear to be good Catholics? Maybe you are." Yes, maybe they are; however, as the next question probes, what if the outside doesn't match the inside?

How Did Life Inside Compare to the Expected Image?

The most common answer is: "It didn't," meaning life inside was contrary to the image expected and its associated assumptions or messages. Descriptions of the inside might be that it was:

- violent, chaotic
- perverse
- shaming or shame-filled
- cold
- rigid, controlling
- lonely

When there's a mismatch or dissonance between life inside the family and the expectation to appear a certain way, members suffer; stress-induced impaired coping behaviors increase. It is crazy-making to feel pressure to look good, especially as children, while the truth about life inside was that we were anything but good. This leads to the final related question:

How Did You Cope with That Mismatch and the Feelings It Aroused?

Common ways of coping include:

- using alcohol or other drugs (escaping)
- isolating
- rebelling/refusing/arguing/getting into trouble (blaming)
- complying while hating myself for doing so (often the pathway to self-harm)
- focusing on a single member who seems to have the worst problems (fixing)
- achieving and working extra hard to be the best (distracting)

Take some time to consider these questions. Write down or dictate your answers. When you conduct such an inquiry, especially if you can do so with members of other families who have been affected similarly, you'll be forming the basis of your personal recovery from SIIC. And, remember, when even one member of the system, *you*, begins this change process, the entire system shifts toward wellness.

As members struggle with life in the wounded family environment, they experience increasing pain and powerlessness. Employing impaired coping methods (fixing, escaping, blaming, distracting) perpetuates the powerlessness. The system develops an identified patient (IP) upon whom the members focus and try to change. Usually the IP contributes to being seen as the problem by exhibiting problematic behaviors. For example:

Married parents of two sons, Kevin and Jen live just south of San Francisco in a middle-class suburb. The boys, Dylan and Jason, are eleven and eight. Dylan is an imaginative, inward sort of kid with several very close friends. Jason is like a tornado who roars through every environment he encounters. A typical dinner conversation:

"Guess who called today," Kevin looks at his wife as he's chewing.

"Let me guess," Jen quips. "The dean of boys."

"Bingo!" Kevin booms. Dylan starts squirming in his Batman pajamas. Jason had not yet come to the table, refusing to get off the TV and his neon bean bag chair. Neither parent wanted to confront him lest a tantrum ensue.

"What did he do now?" Jen kept things going.

"Alright, get this. He threw a full container of milk into a crowd of students, soaking some poor girl it hit on the head."

Jen sinks a bit in her chair. "I can picture him doing that."

A silence falls over the table as everyone digs a little deeper into their plates and themselves. After a pause:

"So, what are they going to do to him this time?" Jen wonders.

"Week suspension," Kevin says finally.

"I can't stay home from work with him," Jen shrugs.

"Well I certainly can't. I've got the presentation Thursday."

"I guess I can go in late most of those days," Jen gives up.

Dylan slinks away to play Minequest.

In this system, Jason serves as the identified patient. He commands a disproportionate level of family resources, particularly attention. He is a "blamed one" as outlined in the previous chapter, frequently in trouble and coping with life in the wounded system by remaining in trouble. He can't bear not to be the center of attention, even though most of that attention is critical or punitive. Older brother Dylan slinks further into himself and his friends. A classic escapee, within a few years Dylan spends most nights at his best friend's house about a mile and a half away. Kevin, the dad, is a distractor/super-provider, his job being the most important thing. He expects the family to understand that and accommodate his work life. He copes with the pressure of his intense job and empty emotional life by using alcohol and pain pills, a practice he began as a teen. He is at high risk for addiction, if not already there. Jen, the fixer, will serve, smooth, and soothe Jason (and her husband) by any means she can come up with. She'll make excuses for him, put out cover stories and alibis to get him out of trouble, write his term papers, and minimize the trouble he's made in her reports to Kevin. She'll continue her long-established coping style from childhood by eating, becoming obese by the time the boys are twelve and nine. Both parents will try a myriad of corrective methods for Jason including all three outlined on the following pages: punishing, monitoring, and providing. The cycles deepen and repeat.

The pain in the system and everyone's worsening mental and physical health are overlooked in the IP model in which the focus rests on the identified patient.

The pain in the system and everyone's worsening mental and physical health are overlooked in the IP model in which the focus rests on Jason.

This family did recover, but only when the parents addressed their own impaired coping (Mom's fixing, Dad's substance abuse and emotional absence, Dylan's retreating). Eventually, with Kevin clean and sober seven years and Jen's eating under control and return to a healthy size, at seventeen, Jason attended a year of wilderness treatment and therapeutic boarding school followed by four successful years of college.

When problematic young adults in treatment are asked what their family members have tried to straighten them out, their answers won't surprise:

- Send me away
- Take away my _____ (cell phone, freedom, car, computer)
- Bribe me to be good
- Yell, lecture, direct me

Importantly, when these same young people are asked what they wish family members had tried, they say two things: "I wish they had trusted me to figure things out" and "I wish they wouldn't look to me to solve their anxiety about me." This last statement has very important implications for our work as members of wounded family systems. It suggests that we would be helping our problematic loved ones by seeking solutions for our worries about them that don't involve them changing or being different. This is at the heart of family member and system health: loving detachment from the detail and the drama of others.

WHAT WE'VE TRIED

Consider the various methods you have tried to change or fix a problematic loved one. Compare these with the families described in this book.

Generally, efforts to "fix them" come in three forms: *punishing, monitoring*, and *providing*. Punishing involves taking things away, withholding resources, and inflicting physical or verbal pain. Monitoring describes keeping track and "snoopervising," as a wife of a secret drinker once described it—a cross between snooping and supervising. Providing includes giving, soothing, smoothing, and serving. Examples below.

Punishing

Taking away cell phones, computers, cars, car keys, house keys, doors on rooms, various privileges (driving, watching TV, playing video games), freedom (to leave the house, to stay out with friends), opportunities to attend special events (concerts, parties, dinners out, dates, vacations, trips). Withholding affection, attention, time, and physical presence.

The other form of punishing involves verbal or physical violence: yelling, hitting, throwing things, breaking down doors, damaging vehicles, disposing or destroying property/possessions, changing the locks, or other forms of retaliation for harms done.

While none of these punishments is necessarily wrong, punishing methods reinforce the identified patient structure in the family; when that's in place, everyone gets sicker.

Monitoring

You've tracked their whereabouts, checked their student portals (starting in middle school or earlier), searched backpacks and drawers and pants pockets, read their diaries and text streams (more tech savvy parents divert their kid's texts to the parents' cell phones), viewed their bank account and credit card activity, confirmed or refuted their reports about their whereabouts by asking others if they were really there, staked out friends' or lovers' homes, installed nest cameras and viewed the recordings, recorded and read odometers to determine how far they've driven, and hugged them in order to smell their breath or clothing.

Measuring, monitoring, surveying, investigating, snoopervising, and their related behaviors, while providing what may seem to be necessary information, also reinforce the IP setup in the system. Covert behavior becomes more common. Now even the supposedly healthy ones are sneaking around and hiding their behavior.

Providing

"The road to Hell is paved with good intentions," captures a key element related to providing and enabling (explained later in the chapter). This applies to various efforts family members undertake to straighten out, help along, or give answers to problem family members.

Common providing includes: researching and suggesting clubs, teams, schools, therapists, groups, treatment centers, volunteer jobs, and employment options; signing your loved one up for any of the above; driving them places, especially when it involves waiting for them; giving money you know will be used in ways contrary to what you intended; setting them up in housing or college when all the evidence suggests they are not able to successfully manage such. More extreme examples include giving cars, boats, and plane tickets, or even building a wing onto the house in a desperate attempt to make things better or make them happy.

Thinking about the providing list is tricky: many of you are saying "Well, aren't we supposed to help?" Or, "What if they couldn't do that without my help?" These are valid questions. The next section will clarify the difference between necessary helping and disabling enabling.

RESULTS WE'VE OBTAINED

Consider the results you've obtained from various fixing methods. Most people who read this book have employed punishing, monitoring, or providing well into their loved one's young adulthood, and it is likely these haven't worked. Perpetuation of the cycles of loss, pain, and systemic distress are the results typically obtained. These cycles have been worsening over the years.

More importantly, employing these reactive methods makes everyone sicker with stress-related physical conditions, anxiety and depression, compulsions and obsessions, or worsening substance abuse or addiction.

What Keeps Us Coming Back?

We keep trying for two main reasons: First, the Lies That Bind, as outlined in chapter 3, have held us in their powerful grip. Second, for most of us we have obtained occasional good results: sobriety for the addict, periods of family calm, success at school or work for a time, expressions of appreciation for us with related feelings of closeness and being needed, or obtaining their confidence. Such periodic reinforcement of fixing behavior is sticky and powerful: it keeps you coming back and trying again, despite the evidence suggesting success will be unlikely. This operates in the mind in the same way as a slot machine does. Never knowing when or how much of a payoff we're going to get, but with evidence that there will be a payoff, is the most compelling form of conditioning—known as intermittent reinforcement—to which humans are subject. The bigger the possible payoff, without knowing exactly what effort will provide that payoff, will keep one trying for years while overlooking the destructive effects on oneself of doing so.

So, while desired results may be briefly obtained, here is the list of the most common outcomes family members reported in a workshop entitled 'Home for the Holidays: Now What?' conducted in December 2017:

- another round (of relapse, lying, stealing, law breaking)
- broken promises, broken rules
- resistance, defiance, animosity
- hate, rejection
- heartache, despair
- debt
- $20,000 dental bill caused by bedtime tooth grinding
- loss of: hope, health, enthusiasm, motivation, self-care, energy

This list, highly representative of parents and partners of struggling loved ones, shows how fixing through the various methods tried takes a brutal toll on those trapped in the fixing roles. The results are the same whether punishing (withholding resources including love and attention), monitoring (such as snooping, spying, measuring, and metering), or providing (through planning and procuring).

When compulsively fixing, unable to see the harmful effects it produces, one becomes like the rat standing on an electrified grid, pressing the bar to deliver, on a random schedule, the next hit of cocaine. It's time to get off the grid and launch your recovery. The next chapter will show you how to begin.

NEITHER RIGHT NOR WRONG:
UNDERSTANDING ENABLING

What keeps *them* coming back? As explained, we are mammals impelled by conditioning and conditioned responses; however, so too are our problematic loved ones. They are being reinforced in their behaviors by how we respond to them. When we keep fixing in our classic way (punishing, measuring, or providing), they rely on us to do so, even if they don't like it, and repeat the behaviors that pull on us to fix some more. Here's an example:

Sean is fifteen and has been out of control since high school began a year and a half ago. A bright student capable of academic and sports achievement, he prefers viewing screens and hanging out with his "loser friends," as Mom calls them. This group engages in vandalism and petty theft. Sean's father committed suicide when he was nine; his parents had been separated for a year at that time. A single mother with a demanding job in finance, Vivian has tried "everything" to get Sean back on track, including calling the police when he smashed kitchen cabinet doors in a rage over being grounded. His latest behavior involves sneaking out at night to drink and smoke pot. Lately he's been coming home between 4:00 and 5:00 a.m. and waking his mother with various demands such as making him breakfast or calling him in sick to school. If Vivian refuses, Sean has a tantrum: yelling, cursing, blaming her for the loss of his father, and threatening to run away or kill himself. Vivian heard that sons of suicidal fathers are at very high risk for suicidal thinking and acting. She has become conditioned to respond in a way that avoids Sean's tantrums, with an underlying unspoken belief she can prevent him from being suicidal. She put this effort far ahead of her own needs. In fact, she might make him breakfast (maybe offer to take him to fast food on the way to school) or call him in sick or tardy to school. She tried locking her door and burrowing under the covers, but he'd bang on the door and call her phone over and over. She trembled in fear of the tantrum that would inevitably develop, brutalized by her belief that losing him (to runaway or suicide) would not be far off.

Clearly, Vivian and Sean are trapped and beaten up by the ongoing replay of trauma taking place between them. Vivian's own father, Sean's grandfather, was threatening and at times rageful. Sean lost his father to suicide. Now Sean's substance abuse and teen rebellion along with Vivian's high-demand work, single motherhood, and the materialistic cultural pressure surrounding them in Woodside, California, combine to keep things very stuck.

A set of stories, like the Lies That Bind described in chapter 3, holds Vivian and Sean in their stuck positions, repeating violent aspects of the past. These narratives are known as "covert messages." They are rarely spoken aloud in their pure form; rather, they are implied, interpreted, and inferred. For Vivian, the message she receives from Sean sounds like: "I'm in pain. It's all your fault." For Sean, he interprets his mother as though she's saying: "I'll do anything to avoid your tantrums."

Covert messages reinforce impaired coping and its avoidant or codependent behaviors. The more Vivian believes Sean's pain is her fault, the more she tries to serve, soothe, and fix him. The more Sean believes his mother will do anything to keep him calm, the more he flaunts household rules, assaults her privacy, and escalates his alcohol and other drug use. As they dance in this codependent interplay, the covert messages are reinforced and gain strength. Sean sends the "you hurt me" signals; Vivian confirms his belief she'll do "anything" to keep him calm and protect him from losses and consequences. Under these conditions, it will be nearly impossible to distinguish between necessary helping and destructive enabling.

Examining the covert messages transmitted in the family system (including from ancestral relations) helps differentiate between necessary helping and destructive enabling. By putting the covert messages into words, they begin to loosen their stranglehold. As one speaks them aloud, the aspects of the message that are distorted or untrue reveal themselves. Vivian begins to see that, of course, all of Sean's pain and turmoil can't be her fault. She begins to wonder about the effects of having no co-parent, being on her own battling with Sean, and the absence of a mature masculine presence in his life (and hers). She also recognizes how protecting Sean from losses and consequences (doing his homework, covering for his lateness, accepting his unbelievable excuses) makes it more likely he will continue the risky and violent behaviors she so desperately wishes to extinguish.

In addition to examining the covert messages, looking at the behaviors being reinforced in our loved ones and with ourselves will produce a shift toward clarity. Combining the two processes, that is, articulating covert messages and inventorying the associated behaviors being reinforced in the system (misbehaving and rescuing for example), begins the process of differentiating between helping and enabling.

The most destructive form of enabling is unconscious, that is, providing help or assistance or protection without considering the effects of doing so. Vivian could ask herself, "If I call him in sick again because he's hungover, what effect does that have on his drinking and my problem with his drinking?" She would logically conclude that it promotes future drinking.

By fearlessly examining the messages/beliefs underlying the responses to your problematic loved ones, unconscious enabling will be eliminated. You will be less likely to reinforce troublesome behaviors, which will reduce their frequency or intensity. With practice and detachment, you'll condition your loved ones to expect balanced responses from you that neither enable them nor withhold needed help.

THINKING ABOUT TYPES OF DEPENDENCY

Understanding the nature of dependency at play in family relationships further helps distinguish between necessary helping and unconscious enabling. This involves looking at the developmental stage involved, what others expect, how helpers are treated in the dependency relationship, and the level of impairment or illness in those relying on us.

In a family with children, dependency can be defined in four categories:

- Necessary, developmentally ordinary dependency
- Exaggerated dependency
- Hostile dependency
- Chronic dependency

We'll examine each of these, in turn.

Developmentally Ordinary and Necessary Dependency

This involves just what it sounds like. Parents provide for the evolving needs of their offspring in a way that matches the child's developmental level and supports them to advance. Babies get twenty-four-hour care and feeding; toddlers are provided age-appropriate toys and lots of supervision; preschoolers are offered peer interactions, new challenges, and explanations; and so on, through college age. Parents support the children toward emerging adulthood with ever-increasing independence. Helping children move through these stages and advance to the next one describes the most basic and necessary functions of parenting.

Let's move to the more pathological conditions that show up in families wounded by ancestral trauma and/or with mental illness or addiction in their midst.

Exaggerated Dependency

This sort of dependency occurs when a child relies on others, typically parents, to provide for needs that could be taken care of independently. This is invariably present in parent-child relationships characterized by fixing through providing, as described above. This can be as basic as middle schoolers who "can't" put their laundry in the laundry room or teenagers who "can't" put their dirty dishes in the dishwasher (or empty it, *ever*), or it could be as complex as boys like Sean who "can't" do their homework, keep curfew, or get up in time for school. Complicating things, Sean relies on his mother to provide the absent mature masculine energy he needs from an adequate father figure.

To identify exaggerated dependency, first use your intuition. You probably can determine whether your child is capable of some of the tasks that you've been taking care of. Ask yourself what would happen if you didn't. Perhaps the child would stumble at first or even fail in the short term, but wouldn't the child be able to get it done eventually and learn some self-reliance in the process? It's also helpful to find out what other children of similar age are capable of. Al-Anon members are encouraged to say, "I believe you have what you need to figure this out." You can add, "Let me know what you need from me in order to do it." You're not adding that last part to give your child carte blanche to make demands of you; rather, you're demonstrating your willingness to provide necessary help rather than enable exaggerated dependency. Then think over what your child says is needed from you and use it as a basis for supporting a conversation about individuation and independence; in other words, sort out who's responsible for what.

Hostile Dependency

This condition adds a destructive addition to the dependency condition. The child (of any age) relies on and takes from the parents, usually at an exaggerated level, while simultaneously abusing the parents' goodwill, toxifying the household environment, wasting resources, refusing help, or directly causing harm. These assaults might include high levels of entitlement, derogatory comments, the ignoring of important messages and agreements, or being violent toward the self, others, or property. Sean exhibited both exaggerated dependency (purported academic inability prompting his mother to do his homework and other tasks) and hostile dependency (threatening suicide, "hammer calling" his mother, waking her up in a mean-spirited and selfish way, and drinking/using with no attempt to hide this or comply with mother's wishes).

Hostile dependency pulls for punishing and monitoring as outlined earlier in this chapter. These fixing responses intensify the disconnection, disorder, and danger present in a system environment tainted by hostile dependency.

Chronic Dependency

Chronically dependent persons require the provision of care because of a condition such as a disability or illness that prevents them from meeting their needs on their own. This could be the result of a developmental disability; a traumatic injury, especially to the brain or spine; or severe mental illness such as schizophrenia. In chronic situations, it becomes very important to carefully think through what needs must be met by others as opposed to what the person can learn to access independently.

What Keeps Us Stuck?

Once again, it is our beliefs that keep us stuck. Exaggerated dependency is reinforced by the parents' fears of failure for their children. Doing for them what they could do for themselves is believed to protect them from further losses. Hostile dependency involves a form of hostage taking in which the parent knows she's trapped yet believes she must soldier on and tolerate the assaults lest worse losses accrue (suicide, estrangement, incarceration, etc.). The distorted belief is that these losses can be avoided by the parent remaining hostage; usually, the parent's ability to reduce that risk is little or none, though the illusion of being able to control things is powerful and reinforcing. The Lies That Bind (described in chapter 3) including "I'm keeping him alive" and "I owe" are usually in operation in parent hostage taking.

The difference between a mother saying: "Oh crap, she's gonna drink today; I've got to do something." Or "Wow, that's a really strong worry I'm having right now; what are my options to deal with it?" Or "What allies can I call on to help me manage this intense feeling about my daughter?" Or "Is it true I'm as alone with this worry as I feel?" All these latter thoughts help Mom face her fear rather than repeat the classic focus on her daughter's alcoholism. The first thought, about the daughter, perpetuates fear fantasies, powerlessness, and the repetition of classic (impaired) responding. The latter self-view, in William James's terms, expands our sense of the now (mindful presence) and will "dissolve the fear in our minds."

MAXIMIZE YOUR LEARNING

- Describe the family deal, the setup, in your family of origin (FOO) and family of today.
- Ask and answer the questions posed in this chapter to elaborate on the deal.
- Spell out how you participate in the family deal, including the effects of your participation on your loved ones, your health and self, and the family system.
- Inventory the various attempts you've made to change others.
- Consider the results you've obtained from such efforts.
- Name the beliefs you hold that make unconscious enabling possible.
- Put into words the covert messages you receive and the ones you may be sending.
- Identify the type of dependency condition(s) you've experienced.
- Interrupt yourself when your thoughts fill up with "him" or "her" and come back to "I" and "me."
- Most importantly, keep going in this work even if some of what's been described seems unclear or not applicable to you.

The next chapter will introduce the Stress-Induced Impaired Coping (SIIC) recovery method, offering specific examples to change beliefs with sample dialogues to bring alive how to move from Classic responding toward healthy emotional detachment.

· 6 ·

There Is a Solution

Small Shifts Produce Big Results

Build your toolkit for healthy coping to create the changes you need most.

The previous chapters outlined the characteristics of the wounded family environment, the roles members are pulled to play, the forces that keep things stuck, and the perpetuation of systemic turmoil and loss caused by stress-induced impaired coping.

Now, it's time to build your toolkit for healthy coping.

Let's start by preparing for difficult interactions you commonly face. Keep in mind you're developing a practice—a way of thinking and responding to free you from the old beliefs keeping things stuck. You'll learn to protect and promote your serenity, manage difficult or disabling emotions, and lean in to your important relationships to create the highest levels of closeness you and your loved one(s) can achieve.

As with any practice, this takes time. Let yourself be a beginner and fumble around; make mistakes; and, at times, fall back into your old way (we'll call "the Classic"). When you stumble, get back on the horse, regroup, acknowledge your slip, and press on.

It's not easy to develop a new way. Many of us believe we should already know this stuff. Making it more difficult, our culture does not welcome the beginner. In some cultures, the beginner is revered and welcomed. Not so, in our Western world. There's pressure to be right. And, in wounded family systems, being right is as toxic to system health as is alcohol abuse, self-harm, or disordered eating.

In this recovery work, honor yourself as beginner. Show yourself the same empathy for your emerging self as you do for your loved ones when they demonstrate their problems. Usually we're much kinder to others than to ourselves. A key aspect of this practice is kindness: especially toward ourselves.

Let's start by examining how we communicate with our loved ones when we're under stress, feeling pressured or used, or facing an apparent crisis. As explained previously, we respond under such conditions based on our beliefs and the coping methods available to us, which we now will think of as our toolkit. This recovery work involves changing the beliefs that have gripped us so tightly, while simultaneously expanding our response repertoire and toolkit.

This chapter focuses on communication practice viewed across three levels. Chapters 7 through 9 offer additional practices to take up in other areas of your life.

LEVEL I: THE CLASSIC

In the Classic scheme, emotions are triggered, and we react. When our buttons get pushed (remember, family members installed them), there's not a lot of thinking involved; autopilot takes over. We lash out (directly, sarcastically, or passive-aggressively) or pull away. Loved ones respond using their all-too-familiar methods: blaming, baiting, blackmailing (usually emotional), threatening (usually to destroy), or quoting ("you said"). In turn, we feel held hostage, accused, responsible, disappointed, and angry. These destructive, emotionally driven communication schemes repeat for decades. Now we're going to interrupt these cycles.

Imagine the following interaction between a father and his troubled son:

As Dan made the predawn drive to see Jason for the first time in weeks, he recalled the crazy days leading up to Jason going to the forty-five-day residential treatment program. It was so hard to get any help. After Jason was finally admitted, Dan got a few good nights' sleep for the first time in what felt like years. This week, Jason, at nineteen years old, moved into a sober living home (SLE) that Dan has agreed to pay for. Now, on his way to see Jason, do some shopping, and maybe grab lunch, Dan was feeling that familiar ache in his chest. On the phone yesterday, Dan heard what sounded like Jason slipping away from recovery.

"His main focus seems to be tattoos and video games," Dan mumbled to himself, his irritation mounting.

As Dan pulled up to the curb, he knew he needed to calm down: "Okay, smile, be nice," he cautioned himself. But after waiting fifteen minutes, and texting Jason without reply, Dan could feel his smile vanishing. The kid finally hopped into the car, reeking of cigarettes and wearing a Jose Cuervo T-shirt.

"Hey Dad," he said casually, rolling down the window despite it being gray and windy.

"Hi son, good to see you," with an attempt to smile. "Where to first? CVS or Ross?"

"Well, I definitely need cigarettes."

"I thought you quit."

Silence.

"Dr. What's-His-Name prescribed you that Chantix. What happened?"

"Look, Dad, one thing at a time. I'm not drinking, and most people think that's huge. Can't you acknowledge that? Why do you have to hassle me?"

Dan fantasized pulling over, telling Jason to get out, and going home. "At least I'd have the afternoon left," Dan mused without pleasure. "But I can't do that," he realized. "How would he get back if I kick him out. . . . He might relapse if I do that." Similar thoughts of responsibility and doom swirled in Dan's mind.

These thoughts were quickly interrupted.

"Also, where do we stand on getting me a car? I can already tell it's going to be near impossible without one around here," Jason whined.

"Seriously!" Dan exclaimed. "You're thinking about a car already? You've only been in the SLE for a week."

"I don't know Dad, if I don't have a car how am I gonna get to meetings or look for a job."

Less than five minutes into this interaction Dan was in the Classic soup: blood boiling, feeling controlled and trapped, dashed by the reality of the interaction as compared to what he'd hoped for on the way over. Operating in pure Classic mode, the words just started coming out:

"You get in the car, barely say 'hi,' stink from cigarettes, and now you're hitting me up for a car!"

"But Dad . . ."

"But nothing. And seriously! A Jose Cuervo T-shirt! Why don't you just bring the bottle?"

At this familiar point, Jason will respond in one of several ways. He'll invoke one of his persuasion/control methods, any of which has worked in the past.

The veiled threat: "I don't know why you're so surprised, Dad. Without a car I don't see how I can get to meetings and stay sober. They say, 'meeting makers make it.'"

Dan's Classic response would employ sarcasm: "I doubt you're even going to meetings as it is." This could easily be followed by an attempt to shame the boy for his historical sloppiness and procrastination: "What Step are you on, by the way?" This isn't a question, it's a version of the shaming questioning Dan got from his father: "What the hell were you thinking?" was never a real question. Rather, it was the shame-based way of saying: "You're an idiot."

"Don't worry about my Steps, Dad," Jason countered. "Just tell me the car plan."

Or, Jason might try another persuasion ploy:

"You said": "You said you'd support my recovery. I need the car to stay sober." This conjures an implied promise and rests on the idea that Dan is responsible for Jason's recovery—something Dan does believe.

In Classic response, Dan stumbled into negotiation mode—always a trap: "Well, I, uh, never said that would include a car when you're just one week out of treatment," Dan backpedaled. Notice where the power now lies in this interaction.

Jason had another option:

You owe me: "See, Dad, this is so typical of you," Jason poked. "I get on a good track and you break another promise. It's just like when you left." This immediately activated Dan's "I owe" belief (explained in chapter 3 and the Lies That Bind).

Filled with guilt and just wanting the conversation to stop, Dan surrendered. "Well, a car isn't entirely off the table."

This communication pattern is common in systems like these; perhaps you recognize it. As Dan was drawn into the content and details, he couldn't think critically about what was taking place inside of himself or between him and his son. His emotions intensified, especially the feeling of powerlessness. In this state, he had no options other than angry reacting, bargaining, or giving in to unreasonable or impossible demands.

Now, let's shift to a more constructive approach to navigate these emotional interactions more confidently. Again, be a beginner and don't be discouraged if at first it's difficult—because it will be.

LEVEL II: PROCESS NOT CONTENT

In the above example, inflammatory content concerns cigarettes, meetings, and the car. The pull in most parents would be to explain why the son shouldn't smoke, should go to meetings, and isn't ready for a car. The belief underlying this Classic response sounds something like: "I need him to understand that _____"; or "Why can't he just see how _____." There are many ways to fill in these blanks.

When you're trying to get someone to understand or to see, you get smothered in the content; powerlessness and anger inevitably follow. The goal is to detach from the content.

Let's look at the same interaction from a different perspective. In the Classic mode, you get activated and react with little thought; you're on autopilot. Using Level II process methods, you predict the emotions you'll experience and pay attention to how that emotional process unfolds. Rather than address the content or try to get another to understand, speak to what's happening between you. That's what is meant by "the process."

Here is the Level II version:

As Jason got in the car (late, reeking of cigarettes, and wearing the tequila T-shirt), Dan remembered he wanted to avoid confrontation. "Just breathe," he told himself, as he felt the steam rising. "Don't react. Think, then respond." He reminded himself he would feel irritated or powerless at times.

"Hi son, good to see you," with an attempt to smile. "Where to first? CVS or Ross?"

"Well, I definitely need cigarettes."

"Ugh," Dan groaned, hoping it wasn't audible. He recalled paying for the Chantix prescription and Jason's stories of quitting. 'I need to avoid confrontation,' Dan reminded himself as the old feelings of being used and lied to came rushing back. Thinking about his process he observed: 'He and I have such a stuck pattern. In just five minutes . . . BAM . . . we're in conflict and I'm in the soup.'

Pausing and observing when agitated or doubtful is one of the most effective tools.

"Well, maybe some coffee first? There's a Peet's," Dan offered.

When Jason saw he wasn't going to get the smoking lecture, he surprised his father:

"Look, Dad, I know you don't like that I smoke. I'm trying to do one thing at a time. At least I'm not drinking. Most people think that's huge." By avoiding the cigarette detail, Dan retained his ability to think and act outside his Classic pattern with its misery-promoting traps. Now calmer as a result, he no longer wrestled with the temptation to tell Jason to "get out." Instead, he was much more present.

Alas, this sense was quickly interrupted:

"By the way, where do we stand on getting me a car? I can already tell it's going to be near impossible without one around here."

Here's the moment in which Dan must choose between the content and the process—the Classic or something new. The content is the car request, the smoking, the T-shirt, and the lateness. In Level II, we speak to the process. Generally, that concerns itself with one of two questions:

1. What's going on inside me?
2. What going on between us?

If Dan chose question 1, he might have said:

"You know son, I'm having a strong reaction to how it's going right now, and I don't want that to spill out onto you. I've been working on being less reactive."

Pause here to imagine how Jason might respond. There's no right answer but he'd probably slow down.

Dan chose to pursue question 2 and comment on what he saw taking place between them.

"You know son, I think we're on the verge of getting into a very familiar kind of deal. You ask for stuff and I point out why you shouldn't need it or don't deserve it. Or I make wisecracks, lecture, or talk down to you. I'm trying to do things differently today."

Jason had no response to this. He was startled by his father's talk of how he behaves toward him. Given Jason's silence, Dan continued talking about doing things differently:

"Like I said, in moments like these I usually give you a hard time. That keeps things going in a way that never turns out well. I believe we both end up feeling bad and I know it has created distance between us."

Dan paused to see how this was landing on his son. Still quiet.

"I've started working on this in my own program," Dan elected to share. "Do you think there's any chance we could work together to change it?"

Jason may not shift much yet, but you can imagine the shift in Dan that's already taking place: in both examples Dan was interrupting his Classic pattern by speaking about the process either inside himself or between himself and his son. In turn, he was becoming less involved in being right and instead promoting connection. More about connection in the next chapter.

Let's say Jason kept going undeterred:

"I don't know Dad, if you won't get me a car, I don't see how I can get to meetings or look for a job."

Again, Dan was helped by making a silent process observation:

"Hm, he's still coming at me." By observing Jason's process, rather than getting caught in the content (car "yes" or "no"), Dan found some empathy for his son. In turn, Dan became more aware of Jason's pain and noted his son's immature methods of managing or negotiating; he realized it was his job to help Jason with that if given the chance.

At this point Dan could have tried any of the following content-avoiding responses:

Something about what's happening inside Dan: "Well, what I was trying to tell you about a minute ago has to do with the work I'm doing to better understand what goes on with me. I'm guessing after the treatment you've had you're better at talking about emotions than I'll ever be. But right now, I'm having a reaction that could cause a blow up. Does that make any sense?"

Something about what's going on in the interaction: "This isn't fun for me—leaping into the car thing. What do you say we stick with the original plan for right now and see how the morning unfolds?"

Or, something about their shared history: "Like I was saying a minute ago, I don't think I've ever done a very good job of letting you know much about what goes on with me. Usually I'm telling you what to do or saying 'okay' or 'no' to various requests. I hope someday we could talk about that."

With each process comment, Dan moved further from emotional reacting. Whether these efforts produced a shift in Jason is not as important as the relief it provided Dan. In this state, less in the sway of disabling emotion, Dan showed interest in spending time with his son and a willingness to be honest and vulnerable—to be real.

These are the efforts most likely to produce family system harmony: choosing process over content, making oneself emotionally available and personally real while seeking being in connection over being right.

Keep reading and become the parent or partner who can show up, tell the truth, ask for help, and be emotionally available. Show those who rely on you, and want to love you, that you can reflect on your behavior, admit what's not working, and be real.

Key Questions and Techniques for Level II

The process-focused method involves developing a practice to reduce the power of Classic beliefs and their influence upon emotions and reactions. Paying attention to and speaking about the process reduces the risk of getting sucked into the detail or reacting emotionally to the drama of problematic loved ones. Turn your attention to what's going on inside you and between you and them, rather than what they want, what they might think, what they might feel, or what they might mean. Make the priority optimizing the quality of the time spent together. This will form the basis of your effort to deepen and promote connection—which is what we really want, right?

The following questions offer a guide to thinking about process:

1. What's getting activated in me right now and how do I typically react?
2. What's happening between us and how does it usually come out?
3. What's the outcome I want from this interaction?
4. How might I respond to make it most likely that I can attain that outcome?

This probably sounds like a lot to come up with while riding in the car with your son who's stinking of cigarettes and working you over; however, with practice you'll soon find it coming to you naturally.

Let's go back to the interaction. This time Dan will draw from the four questions above to frame his process approach.

"Hi son, good to see you," with an attempt to smile. "Where to first? CVS or Ross?"

"Well, I definitely need cigarettes."

Dan was immediately in it. In a mindful moment he thought, "I'm in it."

Noticing or observing that he was "in it" helped separate him from being dragged "into it." He asked himself question 1: *What's getting activated in me and how do I typically react?*

"OK. He's late. Tequila T-shirt, cigarette stench. I'm annoyed and feeling trapped." He breathed deeply and realized, "This is when I would either snap at him or give him a lecture." Dan saw how snapping or lecturing was driven by feeling trapped. That trapped feeling was brought on by Dan's belief that he must do what Jason wants, a version of the Lie That Binds: "He'll relapse and I'm responsible."

Employing a process-focused way of viewing the situation, Dan thought: "Wow, one minute in and I'm ready to blow." Pausing to notice his thoughts and feelings, rather than be ruled by them, had an immediate calming effect.

Jason noticed that his father wasn't reacting in his usual manner; he expected the lecture, or for critical comments to start as the car pulled out. "Dad are you OK?" he asked nervously.

Dan could feel the shift in mood.

"You know son, I'm feeling a little stirred up right now."

Jason would likely inquire: "What's wrong?"

Success! Jason was sticking his toe into the process water without even knowing it. Dan had several choices at this point. He could create additional pause or talk about his inner thoughts and feelings—probably something that hasn't occurred between these two in quite some time.

Here is what these could sound like:

Suggest taking a pause: "I'm feeling a little stirred up right now. How about we get some coffee and make a list? I saw a Peet's back there."

Describe your inner self and acknowledge that you're operating differently: "I'm feeling a little stirred up right now. I know in the past I've never talked to you much about what goes on inside me. Usually I just focus on you, get angry, and start yelling or lecturing."

"Yeah, you do!" Jason might quip.

It's a little early in our process work here, but imagine if Dan invited Jason into the process examination:

"Could we talk about that?"

We don't know exactly where these approaches will lead; however, unlike in the Classic setup in which the emotions and tension escalated, both men slowed down. Dan was less inclined to lecture or snap, Jason was disarmed and therefore less likely to poke or provoke.

The process method leads into unfamiliar territory that at first might sound impossible to pursue. You might think, "I can't talk like that." Don't despair. With the process questions to guide you and a little derring-do, you'll be reducing conflict and emotional reacting regularly.

A process-method way of responding is guaranteed to produce better outcomes than the Classic.

Back to the car ride. Let's say Jason pressed on as in the original script:

"By the way, where do we stand on getting me a car? I can already tell it's going to be near impossible without one around here."

Now ask question 2: *What's happening between us and how does it usually come out?*

Dan thought about the interaction, rather than the content of car, yes or no. "This is very familiar," he thought. "I'm getting worked!" It came to him like a slap. "And how does it usually come out?" He felt his sap rise. "Well, after I lecture or put him down, I give him what he wants, usually based on some promise he'll do it differently this time." Dan felt awake and alive, almost ran a red light. "Slow down, breathe," he reminded himself.

"Hey, there's a Peet's. Let's stop and make a plan," Dan proposed as he turned into the parking lot. "I'm gonna go the bathroom real quick, be right back." He resisted saying "Why don't you get in line and order for us?" mostly because he didn't want to give Jason his credit card. Dan noticed this and thought: "We have a long way to go in the trust department."

In the bathroom (a great place to think) Dan asked question 3: *Okay, what's the outcome I want?* "It's simple. Spend some time with him, buy some of the stuff I planned, and show that I care." That set up an easy answer to question 4: *How might I respond to make it most likely that I can attain that outcome?* "Easy, Dan thought. What I'm doing so far is working. I'm clear about what I'm up for today with him." Dan next thought about what he knew he wasn't up for: "I'm not available to be worked. I didn't come down to discuss buying a car. I'm allowed to want to enjoy our time together or at least have it be respectful."

Dan strolled out of the bathroom with an emerging sense of confidence and relief.

"You know son, we might have gotten off to a bumpy start, or maybe it's just me. I'm glad we stopped for a few minutes. I'm getting a latté, what do you want?"

As they sat with their coffees at an outside table, Dan noticed that things had slowed down. "My goal is for today to be fun and kinda' light. What about you?"

"I don't know, Dad, I really need a car, man."

Dan was getting clearer every moment: "Well, Jace, I didn't come down planning to do the car thing. I don't really want to discuss it yet," he said softly.

Jason harrumphed.

Dan chose to say something about feeling worked: "Well, son, I get that the car is important and you want one now. I need to tell you that I'm feeling pressured and that isn't fun for me."

Alternatively, Dan could have spoken about his preferences for the day: "You know, when I drove down, I decided I wanted to focus on being with you and getting the stuff we planned. Right now, I'm not up for more than that."

Or, Dan could have jumped into the car content but focused on his position in the car deal. This is a bit more advanced: "I know how important getting a car is to you. Truth is, I'm not ready to be back in a car deal with you yet. I end up monitoring your use and your whereabouts and worrying about the money and legal stuff—I'm just not there yet."

Level II Summary

One might worry that shifting the focus to process would lead to the other person to feel ignored or put off; paradoxically, attending to the process by speaking to internal states and emotions reduces conflict and produces trust and closeness. Loved ones don't feel lectured or controlled; rather, they appreciate being invited into an adult-adult relationship. When speaking about what's taking place inside you, the other person can't really argue. "You're not ready for a car," produces an argument: "Yes I am!" Instead, when Dan said *he's* not ready to be in a car deal with his son, although Jason didn't like that, he really couldn't argue. Dan was gently insisting that his position mattered from a financial, emotional, and personal standpoint. Jason's demands and readiness were no longer the top consideration. This freed Dan to step away from the car question and back to the visit itself.

The process method takes practice. Expect to fumble around for a while, drift into the Classic, and then recover. It will be important to permit and ask for "do-overs" when something doesn't go right. Try saying: "Hang on, that came out more harshly than I meant," or "Wait . . . what I'm trying to say is . . ."

The process method values kindness: to oneself and your loved ones. Staying in the content generally produces conflict and corrodes closeness. Set an intention to attend to your needs and place being in connection over being right. This forms a cornerstone of SIIC recovery. When you concern yourself with your reactions and show concern for their effect on others, your loved ones will notice and move toward you. A new and improved connection becomes possible.

> When you consider your reactions and show concern for their effect on others, your loved ones will move toward you.

More about connection in the next chapter.

LEVEL III: USING SELF-AWARENESS

The self-awareness level adds an additional layer of detachment to protect against being taken over or overreacting. This approach involves increasing awareness about the beliefs you hold about your loved one(s) and questioning your degree of responsibility for them. When these beliefs are activated or challenged, Classic reacting inevitably follows. Recognizing these beliefs, their origins, and the circumstances under which they exert the greatest power to trigger regretful reactions will shake their destructive grip.

Consider this mother-daughter pair:

Dolores was leaving the busy shopping center, regretting having worn the wool pantsuit. It was hot, and she still had to get to the dry cleaner.

"Mom, I just got fired and I didn't even do anything."

Dolores moaned as she read the text. "I just want her to be happy!"

Jessica had been difficult since her first days. Born at just thirty-two weeks, she spent her first three months in incubators and hospitals, with Dolores permitted to hold her for just a few hours a week. Junior high and high school seemed like a never-ending series of emergencies, treatment attempts, blowups, and disappointments, punctuated only by occasional moments of calm or feeling close. Somehow the college years didn't seem quite as turbulent, something settled. But in the last year, since Jessica's graduation and move to San Diego, Dolores had felt all the familiar feelings from the early years flooding back: responsible, scared, angry, and burdened. Jessica was quite willing to offer plenty of blame to reinforce Dolores's view of herself as at fault.

"Speak to what's happening between us," she told herself, remembering to stay out of the content as she'd been learning in the SIIC recovery Level II Process method. "Choose being in connection over being right," had recently become her mantra.

She and her husband had discussed just last night how vulnerable they felt to the threat of returning to the Classic position, in which they tried to figure things out for Jessica and show her the better way. They'd learned to recognize the trap they fall into when thinking, "I just want her to _____" or "She just needs to _____." Dolores thought about all the ways she could complete that sentence. "I just want her to: accept she has an illness, go to a therapist, take the right medication, go to AA meetings, get job coaching, go to graduate school, apologize to her grandfather, choose better boyfriends, . . ." The list could go on for pages.

The lists are powerful: First, the ideas and plans are good and useful; they likely would work. Second, dropping the list feels like giving up on our loved one.

Don't give up on the list. Instead, notice that it is you who is holding it. People do what's on their own list; not what's on someone else's. Think of the specialized wristbands you see modern football quarterbacks wearing. They have a record of various plays the quarterback could call during the game. The quarterback can see these when he needs them most: on the field and in the huddle. The metaphor applies to our loved ones, too. They're only going to change the aspects of themselves that they've made it a project to take up—that is, what's written on *their* wristbands.

We need to tolerate the difference between what's on their project list and what we wish their project would include.

Here's an example:

An anxious, troubled father, scrambling to find housing for his lifelong dependent fifty-year-old, said to me: "She's just three credits short of a bachelor's degree." This short statement captured a force that had been holding this retired surgeon and scratch golfer in exaggerated dependency since his daughter was a teenager. He believed if only she'd finished her degree, all would be fine.

"How long have you been saying that?" I asked gently.

He hung his head and said: "Almost thirty years."

"It doesn't seem like that's high on her list," I said. "What does seem important to her?"

"Drinking, I guess," he said morosely. "Her mother was the same. She died twenty-five years ago."

In his SIIC recovery work, this father identified the effects of his belief in the college story. It:

- held him in the dependency loop;
- protected him from thinking critically about how he responds to his daughter;
- separated him from facing his daughter's alcoholism and apathy; and
- shielded him from considering losing his daughter as he had her mother.

To practice Level III Self-Awareness, make an inventory of your beliefs and their destructive effects. This will make possible more effectively responding to your loved ones, reducing the likelihood of impulsive reacting. Of all the things you (as a parent or spouse, or adult child) can do in a dependency relationship, changing how you think and respond will produce the most meaningful results. By doing so, you foster the conditions under which your loved ones will most likely make their own list—that is, they will define and take up the project of their recovery and their lives.

Recall Dolores and the text from her daughter about being fired described above. Before leaving the parking lot, Dolores remembered one of the earliest teachings: Pause when agitated or doubtful. "That's right," she thought. "I don't have to respond instantly just because it's a text." Nonetheless, memories of suicide attempts and death threats returned in a torrent.

"I don't think she can handle it," pounded in Dolores's head as she got into her car. "This is where I have to do my work."

Dolores's thought, "I don't think she can handle it" offers a window into an important technique to drive the shift from other awareness to self-awareness: Notice the pronouns being used, including he, she, you, I, we, him, her, me, us. When thinking "I don't think *she* can handle it," restate the thought substituting "I" or "me." Perhaps change it to "I don't think *I* can handle it." Next, think something like: "What would I need in order to handle it?" or "What have I done in the past . . . and how has that worked?" While this thinking will be unfamiliar and uncomfortable, it will produce a shift away from Classic thinking and reacting, supporting one of the main SIIC recovery objectives: "anything but the Classic."

To shift from other-focus ("she can't handle it") to self-focus, Dolores could ask herself something like:

"What's stirring me up?" "What do I need to handle this?" "How can I best handle this?" or "What do I need to handle this differently than I've done in the past?"

As she shifted her attention away from her daughter and toward herself, Dolores experienced the benefits of detachment from Jessica's details (job loss and upset). She was able to loosen the grip of her distorted beliefs, avoid reacting from fear, and make an offer in support of connection. Read on to see how she got there.

Key Questions and Techniques for Level III

By learning about ourselves, the self-awareness approach makes it easier to manage difficult encounters or conversations. The covert assumptions, disabling beliefs, or stories we hold are related to the "Lies That Bind" (as explained in chapter 3). They live in our minds outside conscious awareness. Part of their power lies in the fact that they are partially true. They are not delusions; however, they are always distorted in a way that exaggerates our sense of responsibility and hold us in the Classic ways of reacting.

The Lies That Bind and related beliefs, particularly about others and their needs, represent the single most powerful force perpetuating hostile and exaggerated dependency in the family system. When we put them into words and question their truthfulness, we loosen their stranglehold and shift the system toward health.

Level III Self-Awareness questions (see worksheet in chapter 8):

1. What is the underlying belief being activated in me?
2. How is that belief or story influencing how I tend to see things, how I feel, and how I respond?
3. What's the posture, or stance, I want to take in this relationship?
4. Given that stance, what am I available for?

Let's go back to Dolores's parking lot moment. She had worked on her Lies That Bind Inventory (chapter 8) and unearthed the following underlying beliefs:

I'm keeping her alive.
I owe her.

As Dolores steadied herself, she decided not to leave the parking lot just then. "Here's my chance to do it differently," she thought (rather kindly) to herself. She got out of the car and walked toward some tables outside a frozen yogurt shop.

"It's been true for so long that whenever Jessica is in any distress, I think she's gonna vanish or die." She then asked herself: "Was there anything she said in that text that's even close to her life or safety being threatened?" Of course, Dolores knew the answer was "no." She was also learning about the forces inside her that pull her to hear Jessica's communications as life threatening. Slowed down a bit, she thought of returning home to talk things over with her husband.

It wasn't that long ago that Jessica was hospitalized, twice, for pill overdoses that were understood to be suicide attempts. In the second one, Dolores found her daughter delirious and stumbling, and she called 911.

An empty bottle of sedatives and a three-quarters-empty vodka bottle were in her daughter's car. Paramedics whisked her to the ER; her stomach was pumped. Doctors said if she had been left alone, she probably would have died.

If you've saved a loved one or witnessed a loved one at death's door, it's nearly impossible to shake the belief that you are responsible for keeping that person alive. It's important to honor that experience and the way it powerfully reinforces the "I'm keeping her alive" belief.

Dolores had done some grief work to mourn the loss of the ideal daughter she pictured when Jessica was little. The trajectory Jessica had moved along was very different from what any parent would picture or want. Stitches for cutting herself at age thirteen, wilderness treatment at age fifteen, anorexia treatment at age seventeen, and then, miraculously, the four okay years of college.

"I said when I completed the last family workshop: 'I'm not going back,'" Dolores reminded herself, recalling waiting up at night with her husband and cell phone inches away, wondering whether Jessica would come home okay.

"We're not going back to serving as her caretakers. We're not going back to the infinite worrying," they encouraged each other. They knew they had to find an alternative to the fixing, rescuing, and clutching at straws of hope.

Now, at risk of being in the sway of "I'm keeping her alive," Dolores thought about how to respond. "What if I did nothing for a while," she mused. "This is not a 911" ("yet," added her cynical voice). "Plus, she's in San Diego and I'm in San Francisco. I've got to stay real about the limits of what I can and can't do." Dolores learned that for many years she had given herself superpowers in her daughter's life: Super Job Obtainer, Super Boyfriend Chooser, Super Mind Reader, Super Future Predictor.

She then asked herself a super-important question: "Since I'm not a superhero, what am I, and what am I available for?"

She relaxed the grip of "I'm keeping her alive" by reminding herself of her powerlessness to protect Jessica and how this wasn't a life-threatening situation despite her fear.

Dolores next turned her attention to the second belief on her list: "I owe her." Dolores had really struggled with this one and saw how important it would be to reduce its power. There was a turbulent three-year period when Jessica was ten to thirteen years old, in which she and her then-husband were battling. He'd move in, he'd move out. They'd yell and fight, then make up and go on a long vacation with Jessica. During this period, Dolores used much more alcohol than she ever intended and was arrested for DUI on her way home from a reconciliation dinner meeting with her husband that went very badly. She missed many of Jessica's basketball games and fell asleep one evening when she was supposed to be at the seventh-grade talent show (which Jessica won). The relentless question: "How can I ever make that up to her?" often tormented her.

At the same time, Dolores has been encouraged in her personal work to honor and appreciate the steps she has taken to show up more reliably for Jessica. She found the strength to divorce Jessica's father, an untreated alcoholic. She drank only in moderation for the past ten years, paid for Jessica's college, and had now begun to address her codependency.

Dolores was now ready to define her posture (stance) with respect to Jessica:

"I can't change the past," she told herself. "What I can do is show up for a relationship with my daughter, pursue connection with her, and be honest with myself about my limits."

Dolores next put into words what she would be available for with Jessica:

I'm available for an adult-to-adult mother-daughter relationship that's as close as we can create. We've had losses and rough times—that needs to be acknowledged. I'm available to listen unless I'm feeling manipulated, pressured, worked, or like I'm receiving a hostile download. Also, I get to manage what I listen to and for how long.

She also spent a few minutes reviewing what she knows she is not available for:

I'm not available to find her a new job or be her job coach. I'm not qualified. I'm not available to receive an emotional evacuation of her uncertainty and distress if it comes at me as an attack or threat. I will no longer be held hostage by my fear or guilt.

Armed with these points of self-awareness and determined to resist the Classic, Dolores responded to the text:

"Sounds really stressful, Sweetie. I have Pilates till 7. I could talk for a few by phone when I get back home."

She received a surprisingly non-urgent reply:

"Can't talk more now, Mom. Gotta go. I'll call tonight."

A Level III Look at Dan's Story

Like Dolores, Dan had examined his beliefs about Jason. He saw how feeling powerless fed his irritability and short temper with his son. In that state, he'd been unknowingly keeping the cycles of exaggerated and hostile dependency going. He named the following distorted beliefs (lies) as his main drivers:

> *I'm responsible for Jason's recovery.*
> *He'll fail or relapse if I don't provide whatever he needs.*
> *I owe him because I let him down (the divorce, being away on business, my new wife's open dislike of him).*

Watching Jason add what looked like ten packets of sweetener to his latté from across the busy cafe, Dan realized how he's more comfortable thinking about someone else's life and needs than his own. Though not proud of that awareness, he saw how operating this way kept him glued to Jason's and others' problems (real and imagined).

As Jason walked toward the table, Dan thought about his beliefs and examined their accuracy. He spotted the distortions. "How can I possibly be responsible for Jason's recovery?" he thought. "'I can't get him sober or keep him sober or make him relapse. If I could, I would've made him sober years ago!"

As Dan saw the distortion in his mind, he became clearer: "Jason's recovery will only work when it's his project, not mine."

Dan used this idea to clarify his stance with respect to his son: "I'm not giving him any money," he said sternly to himself, "and, I'm not going to be around him if he's high or drunk or extolling the virtues of the marijuana lifestyle." Dan smiled inwardly as he realized he could legitimately set these limits.

As Jason pulled out the chair across from him and sat down, Dan said, "You know, when I drove down, I thought through what I want for today. To spend time with you, most of all, and to get some of the stuff we talked about. I'm not up for more than that right now."

Let's say Jason responded, "But, Dad, you said you'd come down and help me out today. I can't do this recovery stuff without a car. I'm telling you."

This was Dan's challenge moment to use self-awareness. He flashed on the Classic response and knew it would only lead to a blowup. He rejected that option. He then chose to say something about the position he's in:

"It's true, son, I am here to help you out." Dan paused, collected his thoughts, and took a breath. "I've put a lot of energy over the years into trying to get you to do things or to see things in a certain way—my way. That was part of the Dad job. But I see that no longer works."

Jason was quiet.

"I get it now," Dan continued. "I can't keep you sober. I can't get you to stay in the SLE, quit smoking, go to college, or any of the other great ideas I have for you." Dan chuckled at "great ideas." He showed Jason he was trying to keep it light.

"You've always had a lot of them," Jason jabbed somewhat playfully.

"If I could've gotten you sober," Dan went on, "I would've done so a long time ago. But now I get it. Your recovery must be yours and you're in charge of it. And in many ways, it looks to me like you're doing a great job."

"Do you really think so?" Jason said in a near whisper.

"I do, son," Dan softened, too. "I know it isn't easy."

A surprising calm came upon them. Dan kept quiet.

"Actually, Dad, it means a lot to me that you came down. I can get rides from friends or take the bus for now." Dan's jaw dropped (internally) as his son dropped the car demand.

Dan paused a full beat. "I'm here to back you in this process and I'm glad to do so. I'm also working on how I think and talk about things, especially in my relationship with you. Maybe if I keep it up, one day I'll no longer be a control freak."

They both laughed, their bellies full of love and lattés.

KEY TAKEAWAYS

Consider the beliefs held by the parents described in this chapter. Notice how sticky they are and how they support maintaining responsibility for their offspring, regardless of how old they are. Each belief has a cover story, such as, "She just needs three units to graduate," or "She can't survive losing another job." Beneath the cover story is a powerful (but faulty) assumption: "I should be able to fix this," or "I am responsible."

Three approaches to engaging more effectively with loved ones during a challenging encounter have been laid out. In Classic mode, emotions are activated, we lash out, shut down, exert control, or invoke the Brutal Bs: blame, bargain, berate, beg, bribe, blackmail, or blather.

Using Level II Process methods, conflict is reduced by shifting away from the content and speaking to what's happening in the moment: inside us or between us and our loved ones. We ask ourselves questions such as, "What's going on inside me?" or "What's going on between us?" We place talking about the process ahead of dealing with the content. We avoid the more complex content discussions and decisions until *we* are ready—regardless of how ready *they* seem or claim to be.

Level III self-awareness reduces the power of the long-standing, sticky beliefs perpetuating what become decades of exaggerated and hostile dependency. Examine the harmful effects of holding these beliefs and question their truth. Develop a stance, or posture, to free yourself from their grip by determining what you're available for and not available for in the relationship. Allow the possibility that you can't effect the changes in them you've wanted for years. These methods combine to make possible healthy emotional detachment—not from the people you love, but from the detail and the drama that makes you sick and keeps the system stuck.

Of all the things a family member can do, employing the SIIC recovery method creates the conditions under which it's most likely loved ones will make a project out of their lives, their futures, and their recovery. We are then in much less danger of making things worse, perpetuating the cycles of illness and loss, and we can freely declare: "My serenity will no longer be conditional on the behavior or the mental health of anyone else, including my children."

Learn to promote and deepen connection in an active way. Build a personal toolkit of serenity-promoting practices to make healthy detachment possible and satisfying. Join with like-minded others who "get it" and who can walk you through doing things differently.

The next chapter offers specific methods to deepen the recovery work.

This is an exciting moment—at the crossroads of the recovery journey. I hope you'll take the plunge; set aside your skepticism; and, as William James said, "dissolve the fear in your mind," and keep going.

Touching It with Love

Choosing Connection over Being Right

Tough love is about as good as tough steak.

BRITTLE CONNECTIONS: ONE FAMILY'S STORY

$\mathcal{S}$tacey and Philip came to therapy after their most distressing encounter with their seventeen-year-old daughter to date. "She looked horrible," Stacey wailed. "Her makeup was crooked, her hair was disgusting, and that ridiculous net pantyhose, it was torn on top of everything else." Philip began sobbing softly. They had been on a crisis ride with this girl for the past year and a half. Following a 911 nightmare that included a heroin overdose at seventeen, Yvette had gone to a thirty-day program. Things seemed stable for a while, then, bafflingly, she stopped eating and dropped to ninety-nine pounds. A former soccer powerhouse and straight-A student, she now spent her days avoiding everything, especially food. A heart-wrenching intervention with lots of threats and crying produced an agreement to go to a three-month program, "but just for one month," she insisted. "I'll run away after that if you don't let me out and you know I mean it."

During that treatment course, which lasted for more than one hundred days, Yvette used the staff's help to end what had become a toxic and degrading relationship with a nineteen-year-old boyfriend who encouraged her to "dance for tips" at a gentlemen's club in Southern California. She let her parents read the letter she sent to this man insisting he leave her alone "from now on."

"She seemed so proud of herself back then when she wrote to What's-His-Name," Stacey recalled. "How on earth could she go back to that?"

"I know," Philip added. "I wish I could kill him. I should've that time in the driveway." Dad was referring to the day about six months after returning from the hundred-day treatment that he and Stacey found syringes in Yvette's purse that she left in the guest bathroom.

"I know I can't stay here any longer," Yvette immediately said upon learning her parents had discovered she was using. "I'll leave now." She began crying as she stuffed underwear and socks into a ratty old blue denim tote bag Stacey had always hated.

The parents hadn't yet begun to decide what to do about the needle discovery and were caught totally off guard when the old boyfriend showed up in a fifteen-year-old Toyota compact belching smoke from its rusted tailpipe. And, as fast as their daughter hopped into that decrepit jalopy, she was gone.

"We knew where she'd likely gone," Stacey said. "Philip spent hours scouring seedy Orange County neighborhoods, finding her one day outside a converted motel. He made the date for the lunch meeting we had yesterday. I guess it's remarkable that she even showed up."

Stacey went on to describe her disgust and shame at seeing her daughter's disheveled condition and could only presume she was erotic dancing and probably prostituting herself.

"I told her I'd meet her for ice cream next Wednesday," Philip mumbled.

"What!" Stacey said. "That's crazy! She's just going to try to get money out of you. And, plus, that would be enabling her and giving her the message we think everything's okay."

Stacey said, "I can't see her in this state again."

Philip said, "I can go by myself."

"Okay, go," Stacey said. "But promise me you won't give her any money."

Philip promised and began a series of weekly visits, painfully witnessing Yvette's slide into worsening states. He never gave her money (though he once gave her a puffy winter jacket) nor told her to get clean or leave What's-His-Name or give any other directions.

Finally, after months of these weekly visits, Yvette said, "Dad, I think I better go back to treatment."

To his credit, Philip didn't hire a brass band or a limo but calmly said, "I bet that's not an easy decision for you. Let me know how I can help."

Yvette did go to treatment in the next few days and stayed more than a year, becoming a volunteer resident at the center and helping many other young women on their recovery journeys. She developed a set of values that rejected all degrading activities and came to see her life and body as precious. The last report was that Yvette had four years of continuous recovery, a stable boyfriend who was working his own recovery program, and a zest for life that hadn't been seen since she was a freshman in high school.

So, what happened?

In short, the parents chose to be in connection with Yvette over being right, as we'll see below. This chapter will demonstrate this strategy and its power to shift a wounded system toward health—regardless of whether problematic loved ones pursue recovery in the short term.

CULTIVATING CONNECTION: FROM THE IMPOSSIBLE TO THE UNCOMFORTABLE

Yvette's parents were tormented not only by their daughter's behavior, but by their powerlessness to make her change. As the family system healing work progressed, they sought to move toward their daughter without compromising their values. Initially held hostage by their fears and helplessness, reinforced by the "Lies That Bind" (explained in chapter 3), they made seeking connection the top priority. This involved spending time with Yvette without condemning, or even commenting upon, her lifestyle choices.

Choosing being in connection over being right, in contrast to all the other ways powerless parents and partners might operate, is the most likely method to create the conditions under which your loved one will face whatever the problem is, seek help, and stay in contact with you.

So, what specifically did these parents do?

At first, like so many, they tried most of the methods outlined in chapter 5 to change her, including sending her away, giving her privileges, and hoping. These Classic responses overlooked the effects the daughter's problems were having on the family members and helped them avoid feeling powerless. As they examined the situation with their daughter in therapy, they slowed down enough to recognize their Classic patterns of responding. They had always believed they must be united in all things—a good practice, although, in this case, one that limited their ability to operate flexibly with Yvette. A key moment in their process occurred when they differed and agreed to differentiate their efforts. When Stacey expressed that she couldn't stand to see Yvette in her degrading lifestyle, Philip stepped up and said, "I can."

While many parent pairs are split by their children and need to work to uphold a more united front, in the family systems work in which this couple was engaged, the united-front policy, as the couple had used it, was modified to facilitate creative problem solving. So, instead of needing to see Yvette together, the father's attitude of "I want to be in connection with her" persisted in the presence of the mother's very different position: "I can't stand to see her like this." By honoring their shared agreement that father would not criticize Yvette or give her money, they remained united while pursuing connection.

Tolerating the Pain

Moving toward connection involves allowing a degree of disconnection. Initially, that's a disconnection from Classic ways of responding and reacting. Many reading this book have been distracted from pain through the fixing behaviors described in chapter 4 (directing, bargaining, brokering, and martyrdom).

As Classic ways of responding are set aside, feelings of powerlessness and fear will increase in the short term. Following is an example of a couple who found relief by connecting with each other after a long period during which their son was a wedge between them:

One last fertility treatment when she was forty made it possible for Caroline to get pregnant and carry the baby to term. A petite white woman raised in Montreal, Canada, she met her six-foot-five African American husband, Arthur, at Duke University. He was a skilled basketball player, she got straight A's and studied twenty-five hours per week. Given racial tensions they witnessed in the South, the couple moved to the San Francisco Bay Area in the early years of their marriage. Steffan's birth was a joyous event, as were the first few years. By high school, he was frequently in trouble, suffered bouts of disabling depression, played video games compulsively, and began hanging out with rough, marginalized kids, including some gang members. Light-skinned with wavy black hair, Steffan could pass for black or white, and, he used this, along with his ADHD diagnosis, to every advantage. As he approached age eighteen, shortly after barely completing high school, the couple was deeply split: Arthur dismissed ADHD as a problem and berated and blamed his six-foot-two, physically adept son for dropping basketball in favor of video gaming and "hanging out." Yelling matches with barely contained violence occurred frequently. Caroline became the young man's confidant, seeing him as fragile, wounded by his demanding father, and needing her to comfort him. While she protected him from his father's anger, the couple became further divided, and she lost sight of the destructive effects of her son's behavior, which were exacerbated by her impaired coping. She was held in the grip of the "I owe" Lie That Binds: for bringing him into the world as a biracial boy who appeared neither black nor white with an aggressive father who insisted, "He's black as Barack; what's the problem?"

The problem had become violence, estrangement, powerlessness, and fear. By the end of his senior year, Steffan was increasingly isolated, substance abusing, and hostile. He provoked what could have become physical altercations with his father. To avoid such, Arthur stayed away as much as possible, sometimes sleeping at his office. Caroline continued to coddle and protect. After a series of violent episodes in which Steffan broke doors and cabinets in the house, he continued to refuse his parents' pleas to get help. They insisted he leave.

He didn't go far, resorting to sleeping in his truck in a friend's driveway.

"I'm ripped up by this," Caroline said. "He can barely fit in the truck, it's freezing out, and he's bored out of his mind." When Steffan came home one afternoon with an arm broken in a fight, Caroline relented and let him stay after taking him for X-rays, a cast, and some pain meds. Arthur was outraged.

"You can't just let him come back," Arthur pleaded. "I can't take it," he threatened.

"What do you want me to do? Leave him on the streets?" Caroline stuttered through tears. "I'm in pain, too, you know."

After a weekend away during which they drew closer to one another, the parents had a powerful realization: neither wanted to return to their home, which was again taken over by their son. They accepted a suggestion to put their energy into connecting with each other and uniting around their needs—one small step at a time.

Make Decisions Based on Your Needs, Not Theirs

A core element in the connection model involves identifying your needs and insisting they be honored and eventually met. You insist they be factored. For fixers eased by serving, soothing, and smoothing, turning the attention toward your own needs will feel foreign. You might even label it as "selfish" and hear a voice chastising you to "never give up" or "remember that's a parent's job," or worst of all "you can only be as happy as your unhappiest child." Take these thoughts and throw them up into the airspace above you. Examine them as distortions, informed by shame-based notions of obligation, disconnection from self, and exaggerated fears.

Instead ask, "What do I need now to be okay?" or "How am I treating myself today?"

Arthur and Caroline saw how the split between them was destroying their marriage. Arthur blaming and berating while Caroline soothes and protects was not going to produce change in the household or help their son. In therapy, they made a list of all their needs and broke them down into each of three categories: "must have," "strongly prefer," or "it would be nice."

They agreed on the following, with the top two being in the "must have" category:

- We will create a home environment to which we want to return—our sanctuary.
- We're not obliged to live with him and witness his apathy and decline.
- We can't force him to accept help or pursue it.
- We won't make him homeless as a primary tactic.
- Arthur's sleep on work nights must be protected.
- The other's problems will become the shared problems of the couple to solve.
- We will seek connection with our son but without tolerating violence or threats.

As the parents moved toward connection, they agreed only to speak with their son about the situation when together, to attend regular therapy sessions and invite him to join (though they knew he might refuse), and to work together in Al-Anon and a parent support group to pursue their list of shared values (above). They used professional help and peer support to walk through this new way of operating. Caroline made good use of such to manage her feelings about letting go of the (impossible) effort to show Steffan the way or straighten him out.

The couple took up a method I have termed "relentless messaging." Choose a single aspect of the problematic situation to address on a nonstop basis. Addressing it simply takes the form of speaking to it whenever it occurs. In this case, they planned to address Steffan's nighttime behaviors that awakened Arthur. He would be told not to arrive home or audibly play video games between midnight and 7:00 a.m. Though it would be painful, the couple agreed that if Steffan breaks this expectation, they will both get up and tell him to leave and return after 7:00 a.m. If he fails to use headphones and the videogaming becomes audible during these hours, they'll both go into his room and confiscate power cords. If he refuses to comply or noise resumes, he'll be asked to leave until after 7:00 a.m., regardless of the hour. If he escalates the problem, 911 will be called.

As you can see, while Philip and Stacey (Yvette's parents) needed to differentiate and separate from each other a bit, Caroline and Arthur worked to move toward one another. Both sets of parents made being in connection a top priority. At the same time, they honored their own needs by shifting their way of operating to factor in and address those needs.

This Is What "Tough Love" Really Involves

Proponents of so-called tough love advocate withholding love or affection, creating enforced separation, or banishing someone you love. Kicking them out as a solution will produce misery for you and an iffy outcome for them, at best. Making someone hit bottom is not only impossible (since the sense of bottom is subjective), it might produce a result or outcome for which you'd never forgive yourself.

Instead, follow the more effective, though potentially more painful (in the short term) SIIC recovery connection method:

1. Make an inventory of what's been tried.
2. List the results of these efforts, particularly around pain, confusion, or disharmony.
3. Determine whether some separation or greater unity with your partner (if any) appears to be in order.
4. Identify your needs: categorize as "must have," "strongly prefer," or "it would be nice."
5. Insist on obtaining the "must haves" and begin work on the strong preferences.
6. Plan small steps toward your "must haves" while placing maintaining connection with all loved ones as high a priority as possible.
7. Partner with allies who will help you tolerate the pain: therapists, friends who "get it" or have been there, group members as found in Al-Anon, or other support groups.
8. Shift away from trying to solve the loved one's problems and toward partnering with the person.

These eight steps begin a loving process that is truly tough. It's based on telling the truth, particularly to oneself. Consider your loved one with empathy as you detach from the detail and drama in that person's life. See this person as sick and needing help while recognizing that help can't come from you; at least not as the very next step. You've tried that.

Pursuing connection involves positive relating by facing the truth about what's true about yourself, your system, and your loved one. You now have words to describe the family deal—that is, the setup you're in with each other, including how emotion gets expressed and by whom. You can describe how you participate in the family deal and its effects: on you, on your problematic loved one, and on the family system itself. As a result, you've begun the painful process of true tough love.

While many have believed that finding the right words to say, suggestion to make, limit to set, introduction to arrange, or amount of money to give or withhold will create real change, these don't exist; however, there are some "magic words" to employ as part of setting yourself free:

"No."

This one-syllable word carries a lot of weight, though many can't make use of its power. In Al-Anon, it's said that "'no' is a complete sentence." Get clear on what you're up for and find the word or words to set a loving limit when you believe that's what's right.

"That won't work for me" and "This isn't fun for me."

These short phrases offer a way to call attention to your needs and your experience. In most exaggerated or hostile caregiving relationships, the attention has been 99 percent in the direction of the problem person. Now, in SIIC recovery, we turn the attention at least half the time to ourselves.

"I'm not ready to . . ."

Again, the attention has been on what the problem person is ready for, what that person needs, wants, thinks, and so on. Let your degree of readiness for what's coming next or being proposed have value and meaning.

"I believe you have what you need to figure this out."

In exaggerated caregiving, you've been covertly sending a message that you don't believe your loved one can solve things, figure things out, get things done, or take command of the important tasks in life. Expressing a belief that the loved one can do it increases the likelihood it will happen.

"I get it."

A powerful interpersonal moment will occur when you say "I get it," followed by an understanding of what you know to be true about the person. You probably don't like that truth; however, you've been battling with it for too long. Example: "I get it. You're going to keep smoking marijuana as long as you believe . . . [whatever it is the person believes about it . . . it helps you sleep, or whatever]."

"This is going to be difficult for you."

This represents another type of acknowledgment. In this case, you reveal that you're able to accept that your loved one faces something difficult but that you believe the ability to handle it is within the loved one's power. Perhaps that's something you've always protected your loved ones from feeling. You empower them with such a statement, and you free yourself from the bonds of their discomfort.

"For too long I've let your needs come first, no matter the effect on me."

There is an entire set of powerful statements like this to draw upon. Acknowledging your behavior from the past and its effect on the dependency condition will surprise your loved one in a good way and help you explain how you're changing. Other versions include:

"I see why you'd expect me to take care of that for you. I've always done so. But I don't think I've done either of us any favors by doing so."

"It makes sense."

"I'm changing. I see that's a surprise to you."

~

Magic words from a father to his troubled daughter: "I'm getting off the roller coaster, and I hope you'll join me soon."

"I'm getting off the roller coaster, and I hope you'll join me soon," the dad said to his twenty-four-year-old daughter at the conclusion of a three-day multi-family relationships workshop. That short declaration sums up the family member project. These words reflect the dad's intention to shift from trapped parent trying to fix the unfixable to the more sustainable posture of embracing connection. "I'm getting off" recognizes his power of self-determination and choice. His daughter can't imprison him on the roller coaster; he has gotten on it of his own volition; he's now aware he can get off. At the same time, he's acknowledged that she may continue to ride it, a fact over which he gets that he no longer has power. Next, he invites her to be with him, promoting connection while acknowledging that he can't force it or make it immediate. He's holding the door and his arms open for the day she finds herself able to get off on her own. In that state they can be truly close.

Many partners and parents believe this is impossible. That is a shame-based belief underscored by the notion that there are truths about us that are too terrible to face. They can be faced, but this is tough. It requires moving from the impossible to the uncomfortable. From fixing to facing. From watching others to looking inside. From an illness orientation to a system focus. From operating solo and keeping things secret to revealing ourselves to allies (often strangers) who get it and have been there.

Changing belief systems requires facing "the fear in our minds," as William James described more than a hundred years ago. As we let the past slip away by refusing to operate in Classic ways, the mind opens to new and creative solutions. In turn, the fear dissolves, we become empowered, and the system shifts toward health and sustainability for all members.

The next chapter will take you step-by-step through an overview of the entire SIIC recovery process.

· 8 ·

"I Just Want ~~Them~~ to Be Happy"

Your *Recovery Action Plan*

Cross out the word "them." It's your job to be happy!

This book has provided examples and tools to release you from the cycles of relapse, loss, and pain of stress-induced impaired coping, the condition that plagues all members of families with addiction or mental illness in their midst. This chapter outlines the step-by-step process to build your personal recovery action plan. Looking closely at your inner self, your childhood history, and the forces that motivate and grip you may generate some discomfort. Therefore, it's best to find an ally or two who will walk with you through the process—remember, like the addicts and mentally ill ones, alone we get sicker.

Keep in mind the twin goals of family recovery: (1) detach from the detail and the drama of your problematic loved ones, and (2) create connection, closeness, sanity, and safety—for you. Never employ so-called "tough love" as the primary strategy, cutting loved ones off, or impulsively kicking them out. You'll only make yourself miserable. At the same time, as a result of doing your work, you may conclude that living together, communicating whenever either of you feels like it, or supporting the loved one's problem lifestyle has become unhealthy and you will no longer do so.

> Never employ so-called "tough love" as the primary strategy, cutting loved ones off or impulsively kicking them out. You'll only make yourself miserable.

The exercises below are designed to evoke memories and feelings in a psychologically safe manner. Bring your wisest, intuitive self to this self-examination. Take breaks, go at a pace that feels steady but kind. Set aside a quiet time and space and get yourself as relaxed as possible through meditation, mindful breathing, or listening to soothing music or a guided meditation. Avoid this work right after a highly stimulating activity, if you are in intense emotional distress, or when your blood sugar is low.

THE FAMILY DEAL

In the SIIC recovery work, the initial focus involves examining the deal in your family, how you participate in that deal, and the effects of that participation: on yourself, your loved ones (including the most problematic), and the system itself. This will begin your shift away from your focus on others and its effects: upsetting emotions; repeated inter-generational cycles of illness and loss; and distraction from personal life purpose, meaning, and joy.

The goal is to begin to put into words the family deal in which you find yourself today. Start by answering the twelve inventory questions, given below, for the family in which you grew up. Then answer the twelve questions a second time, this time from the perspective of your family of today. Included are a few examples of common answers.

Question	Sample Answers
1. How were key decisions made?	Mom + Dad. Mom decided/Dad announced.
2. What were you valued or praised for?	Good grades, appearance, keeping quiet.
3. How were crises managed?	Everyone scrambled. Swept under the rug.
4. What do you wish there had been more of?	Time with Dad. Communication, honesty.
5. What do you wish there had been less of?	Fighting, arbitrary rule making.
6. What image was expected to be portrayed?	We're: Good Catholics, well educated, upstanding citizens, etc.
7. How did life inside compare to that image?	Chaotic, unpredictable, cold.

Question	Sample Answers
8. What do you know about your family today that you couldn't know then?	There was significant mental illness. Parents did the best they could.
9. What emotions are commonly shown?	Anger, sadness.
10. Who gets to show them?	Dad anger; Mom sadness.
11. What emotions are prohibited or discouraged?	Fear, insecurity, doubt; all—emotions should not be displayed.
12. How did you know not to show (certain) emotions?	Was told I was bad if showing that one. Saw others get shamed.

ENVIRONMENTAL CHARACTERISTICS OF WOUNDED FAMILY SYSTEMS

Next consider the six D's and how they might be alive in your family system. Examples are provided. Consider the degree (low, medium, high) to which each one caused problems in the environment. Again, go through this six-question inventory twice; once for the family in which you grew up and again for your family of today.

Question	Sample Answers
Was there Disorder?	Chaos. Out-of-phase development. Parentified children.
Was there Disconnection?	Feuds, estrangements. Members out of touch with themselves.
Was there Deprivation?	Shortages of emotional goodies, developmental nutrients.
Was there Danger?	Risk of: physical violence, sexual intrusion, humiliation.
Was there Doubt?	Poor management of uncertainty. High anxiety in system.
Was there Denial?	Truths (and secrets) about the family can't be considered or discussed. Talking about what's not working was wrong.

COMMONLY ADOPTED ROLES
IN WOUNDED FAMILY SYSTEMS

Chapter 4 described the main roles family members adopt in order to cope with life in the family, including the six D's (disorder, disconnection, deprivation, danger, doubt, and denial). Review the roles given below and identify the ones you most commonly embrace or are drawn toward.

Role	Visible Qualities	Inner Feelings	Represents for the Family	Common Characteristics
Escapee One who leaves or has left the family Drug user/ addict Isolating loner	Creates chaos to which others react Lies, aggresses, charms, withdraws, manipulates Denies impact on others	Shame Guilt Fear Despair	The (unspeakable) problem that is denied and avoided "If only she gets well or comes back we'll be OK"	Inconsistent, irresponsible Self-centered Rigid Blames and denies Invisible or missing
Fixer Chief enabler or codependent one	Maintains control at all costs Rescuer Self-pitying martyr Physically ill	Shame Hurt Anger Guilt Inadequacy	Control Cover-up	Ultra-responsible Detached from self Overbearing Self-righteous Blames and denies
Distractor Superstar Super-provider Entertainer	High achieving and successful Commands attention Does the right thing Judgmental	Shame Inadequacy Fear Overwhelm	Self-worth (the source of pride and accomplishment)	High achiever Sports star Distracts from distress Appears healthy Commands resources
Blamed One Scapegoat or finger Pointer	Hostile Defiant Angry In trouble	Shame Guilt Unloved Hopeless	The visible problem to focus upon	Attracts negative attention and blame Disengaged from activities Supports denial of other family problems

Once you've identified the role you most commonly adopt or are pulled toward, complete the following six-question inventory to understand better the effects and reinforcers of the role. This example is based on the "fixer" role.

Guiding Question	Sample Answers
1. What were the main emotions experienced (as a fixer)?	Sense of responsibility, being in control. Afraid things would become out of control.
2. How did others respond to you in your role?	Relied on me, wanted more. Rejected my help, made fun of me.
3. What were the advantages to playing your role?	Sense of purpose and direction. Belief I was making a difference.
4. What were the costs of playing your role?	Exhaustion. Unavoidable sense things were impossible.
5. What purpose did you serve for the family by playing your role?	Gave hope by seeming I'd never give up. At least the floors and laundry were clean.
6. If you continue in this role unchecked, what will probably happen?	Burnout, fatigue, depression. Drink more or take pills to calm down. End up all alone with stress-related illnesses.

METAPHORS FOR IMPAIRED COPING: "WHAT I BECOME"

Recall the metaphors described in chapter 2. The five questions below are designed to help you find an image for that thing you become when the system is distressing you most. Close your eyes after asking the guiding questions and let the feelings come; an image will likely come to you. Complete the questions based on your family of today, considering the last few years.

Guiding Question	Sample Answers
1. What do I become when things are at their worst?	Punching bag; Rodeo Clown; Toilet; Siri
2. What are the characteristics of that image?	Bruised; ridiculous; filled up; waiting
3. How do others respond to me in that state?	Hit me again; laugh; set me aside
4. What is a healthier/alternative image?	Leader, good friend, dove, dolphin
5. What are the characteristics of that image?	Trustworthy, beautiful, free, smart

IDENTIFYING THE LIES THAT BIND

Beliefs about your loved one and your level of responsibility for their difficulties are the main psychological forces pulling you toward your impaired coping role and into your metaphor. Caught in the sway of these sticky, long-standing, emotionally charged notions, you can't help but respond to your problematic loved one in the Classic way you're now going to interrupt. Identify the lies that grip you from the list below or put into words your personal version. Below are the five most common and the conditions under which they're most likely to take hold.

You're Likely Caught in This Lie That Binds	If You	And/or
I'm keeping him alive	believe he could lose his life believe he'd refuse contact with you have lost someone else to suicide or violent death, including overdose	he has been near death he has attempted or seriously threatened suicide
If only I . . .	explain current problems as result of things you regret or did wrong believe you can find a solution or fix for them	feel blamed or are told you're at fault feel useful or productive when searching for or arranging a solution
I owe	believe your actions from the past have harmed your loved one	your loved one says "you owe me"
I can't stand her discomfort	become agitated or anxious when learning she's uncomfortable can't hold on to the fact that discomfort is a necessary part of recovery and human development	are routinely told by her about ways she's uncomfortable or upset feel relieved when solving her discomfort can't consider your own needs until she's "happy"
He'll relapse if I . . .	believe you can cause his relapse believe there are triggers that can unavoidably cause relapse lose sight of evidence that you can't cause sobriety or recovery	are told or threatened that relapse will occur unless you do what's wanted

When you've identified one or two of the Lies That Bind you, complete the following seven-question inventory to begin to loosen that story's grip. The following example is completed using the "I'm keeping him alive" lie. This inventory can be completed for any of the common lies shown in the table above or for your own version. Create a safe and quiet place in which to do this work.

Guiding Question	Sample Answers
1. What evidence supports my belief?	I called 911 and they saved him last year.
	He confides in me when he's suicidal.
2. What feelings or situations activate the belief?	When I'm terrified for him.
	When I learn he's had a loss or setback.
3. What are the advantages of holding this belief?	Keeps me paying close attention to him.
	Keeps us close—he confides in me.
4. What's the cost or toll of holding this belief?	I lose a lot of sleep.
	It promotes exaggerated/hostile dependency.
5. What would I have to face if I admitted the parts of the belief that are distorted or untrue?	That I could lose him to OD or suicide.
	I can't reliably know where he is or what he's doing 24/7.
6. What would my loved one say about my belief?	"You can't keep me alive, Mom, in all situations."
7. How would it feel to face that?	Dreadful and terrifying but maybe freeing.

At this point, you've made an excellent start. You have words to describe the family deal (the setup) in your family of origin and family of today. You've named the stress-inducing environmental characteristics and the coping style you adopted. You've identified a metaphor for the thing you become when things are at their worst and described some of its characteristics. You next identified the most powerful story, or lie, that binds you to Classic ways of thinking and reacting. You then began to break down the power of that lie by inventorying the evidence that supports it, the parts that are distorted, and what your loved one would say. We ask about this last part to help you see the distortion in the lie. For example, you've believed you're keeping your child alive, to which she might say, "Mom, you can't reliably keep me safe." While that would be sad, it might free you to know that she sees your compelling belief about her as untrue.

Now let's determine: "What constitutes disabling enabling versus necessary helping?" Your answer to this question will be very important.

As explained in chapter 7, the most destructive form of enabling is un-conscious—that is, helping, rescuing, giving, saving, or intervening without wondering about the effects of doing so. When you ask prior to jumping in: "What would the effect of my doing this be on the person and that person's level of dependency?" you reduce the risk of unconscious enabling. The goal is to limit your help to only those things that truly cannot be done by the individual alone, and that you are willing to provide.

Complete the chart below, using the three prompts of "What I've Tried," "Feelings experienced," and "Results Obtained." Some examples are given; use your own experience.

What I've Tried	Feelings Experienced	Results Obtained
Spying, snooping, checking up	Anxious, frantic	Increased distance between us
Keeping her together	Overwhelmed, responsible	Worsening health
Protecting or enforcing his sobriety	Scared, at fault	Relapse: his or mine
Getting or staying busy	Irritated, burned out	Medically ill
Making threats and not following through	Powerless	Greater disregard for my authority
Pleading, begging, bribing	Humiliated	Worsening conditions
Partying with her; gambling with her	Corrupted, guilty	Stolen from
Covering, explaining	Manipulated	Holding the bag
Tiptoeing, walking on eggshells	Vulnerable	Cleaning the mess
Avoiding conflict	Used, ashamed, weak	More conflict
Believing the unbelievable	Betrayed, foolish	More lies and distortions
Having her arrested	Wrong, careless	Paid for lawyers and bail
Using force, fighting him	Angry, injured	Estrangement, hate
Relaxed limits, gave up	Hopeless, lost	More losses: self-esteem, hope, health, money

INTERACTION STYLES: KEEP IT GOING OR INTERRUPT IT

As described in chapter 6, how you participate in both the everyday and more complex interactions with your loved one will either perpetuate the pain and loss or interrupt them. This exercise is designed to take you down memory lane seeking specific instances when your unexamined emotions and beliefs led you to corrode connection or closeness by threatening, confronting, punishing, blaming, dismissing, mistrusting, pulling away, or being unkind. The goal is to use the process and self-aware responses in order to do "anything but the Classic." The table below offers a quick guide to these interaction styles and what they might sound like. Items in brackets are additional examples of the same idea.

They Say	Classic Reply	Process Comment	Self-Aware Shift
I need cigarettes [money, a car, new clothes].	I thought you quit!	Let's not start by talking about something you want	Seems I'm going to get worked to buy stuff. This is not why I came today.
You don't love me.	That's ridiculous. I bought you that BMW.	That's a powerful statement. I'm available to talk about it more if you are.	I worry you believe that. I'd like to understand better what's made you feel that way.
AA and 12 steps are BS. [I'm sick of those stupid meetings.]	You know you have to go if you want to get well. I'm sure you can find one you'll like.	It doesn't usually go well when we talk about your program. I trust you to figure it out.	I should probably get more involved in Al-Anon to have an informed opinion about that. Many have told me to do so.
I could relapse unless you [give me money, let me move in, buy me a phone].	I said I would when you have ninety days of recovery	When you threaten to relapse, you lose me and I can't think straight.	Seems to me if I could make you relapse, I could make you healthy. I can't do either.
You owe me. [You made us move, married that guy, ruined my . . .]	You need to get over it. Things happen in families.	You really want me to know how much that hurt you. When can we talk about it more?	You're right. What happened hurt you. I guess I haven't shown you I understand that.

The responses chosen from the Process and Self-Aware columns, above, promote connection and closeness. They demonstrate your desire to understand rather than make a point or be right. Responding in this way models that you're working on yourself and shows how you're getting real results. Reflecting on your behavior and revealing what goes on inside you grounds you in the moment. The process and self-awareness comments will be naturally available to you as you learn to speak your truth, articulate your needs, acknowledge emotions, and seek understanding. When you say what is true for you, there can be no argument. When you place being in connection over being right, previously unimagined shifts may occur.

SETTING LIMITS: GUIDELINES

While seeking connection is a necessary and essential feature of the recovery process, it must be accompanied by an effort to set limits and clarify the boundaries with your loved one. Particularly when living together or providing financial support, detachment becomes easier when you narrow down what you need from them to a minimum. Start by making a list of everything you want and need from them. Write those down in whatever order comes to mind. Then, and this is the critical bit, categorize each item on your list as follows: "Must Have," "Strongly Prefer," or "It Would Be Nice If."

Here's what it might look like for a parent living with an eighteen-year-old.

First, List Everything	Then Categorize Each
Don't wake me up	Must Have
No drug or alcohol use	Strongly Prefer
Put dishes away	It Would Be Nice
Walk dog when asked	It Would Be Nice
Bathe to not stink	Strongly Prefer
Do your laundry	It Would Be Nice
Take out trash	It Would Be Nice
Treat women respectfully	Strongly Prefer
No guests without approval	Must Have
Don't use cars	Must Have
Don't ask for extra money	Strongly Prefer
Put down the toilet seat	It Would Be Nice

Think of the Must Haves as deal breakers. In other words, you won't continue in the setup as is unless your Must Have condition is met or others are clearly working to meet it. Setting such limits helps your loved one know where they stand and shows you're being thoughtful and fair. After the Must Haves are in place, if your strong preferences are not being met, that will spawn an important conversation about the serious problems to address next.

INTERRUPTING STRESS-INDUCED
IMPAIRED COPING: IT STARTS WITH ME

Wounded systems embrace patterns of operating that perpetuate the cycles of pain, loss, and illness. Members are unaware of these patterns and carry them on for generations. The following chart lists common behaviors, responses, and effects. Look for ones that you recognize in yourself.

What "They" Do	My Typical Responses	Effects on Me	System (Environment) Becomes
Lie	Confront	**Emotional:**	Chaotic
Withdraw, leave	Search,	Anger, Loneliness	Toxic
Neglect, "forget"	Snoopervise	Anxiety, Fear,	Dangerous
Break agreements	Remind, Nag	Rejection	Unpredictable
Drink/Use	Make new	Sadness, Frustration	Cold
Refuse help	agreements		Lonely
Stop meds	Cover for them	**Physical:**	Desperate
Make a mess	Suggest, make	Headaches, body pains	Violent
Steal	appointments	Weight gain or loss	Hostile
Blame others	Plead, beg	Sleep problems	Fraught
Fight, Argue	Clean things up	Stress-related illnesses	
Procrastinate	Correct, Blame,		
	Bargain, Bribe,	**Spiritual:**	
	Cook/clean	Hopelessness,	
	Leave	powerlessness	
		Neglect myself, obsess	

Take a closer look at the second column above, "My Typical Responses." Your loved ones probably respond to these efforts on your part by:

- refusing your help
- continuing to behave badly
- making bigger messes for you to clean up
- blaming, berating, and ridiculing
- ignoring, withdrawing, and other forms of leaving
- resenting you
- assaulting your resources, reputation, and goodwill

Given these, along with the adverse emotional, physical, and spiritual effects on you and the environment that this setup produces, make a practice of employing an alternative set of responses. These form the basis of the SIIC recovery process. Here follows a list of suggested recovery actions, or spiritual actions, and the beneficial effects to expect both for you and the environment. This will be followed by an explanation of specific ways to incorporate these recovery actions.

Alternative Action	I'd Become	System Would Move Toward
Pause, become curious, wonder	Calmer	Connection and inclusion
Listen, ask, reflect	Curious	Acceptance of differences
Show up	Serene	Flexibility, less rigid
Tell the truth	Safer to talk to	Healthier interactions
Ask for and use help	More loving	Warmth
Find allies and join them	Joyful	Wellness
Write, journal	Free	Harmony
Pray, meditate	Hopeful (for me!)	Freedom
Improve self-care		Interruption of SIIC cycles
		Healthier next generation

These alternative tasks form the primary action program of the SIIC recovery methods. They are spiritual in nature; they reflect your values and beliefs about what is right. You have been disconnected from these as you've been pulled deeper into the detail and drama of your wounded system. They serve in contrast to the Lies That Bind, which draw one deeper into the Classic. Employing them draws your attention away from problematic others, their behaviors, and their thoughts. Make it your intention to take these up and incorporate them into your daily life.

Here's a description of each.

Pause, become curious. Pausing simply involves stopping and taking a break to create space or distance. In Twelve-Step recovery, members are encouraged to "pause when agitated or doubtful."[1] A bumper sticker reads "Paws when agitated." That means to seek a dog's calming nature to help you, which makes sense. Dogs don't argue or judge, they elicit compassion, seek our companionship, and accept us in the moment, whatever is going on. Pausing makes possible a similar response from you. When paused, you can become curious about what's going on around you, inside you, and between you and the others nearby. That curiosity is an effective antidote to being taken over or reacting automatically.

Listen, ask, reflect. Listening is an underrated but highly valuable interpersonal method. Unfortunately, when stimulated by anxiety in relationship conflict, it's easy to forget to do so. Be aware of when you think you need to make your point, or "get them to see." By that point in the conversation, the other person isn't listening either. Surprise the person by showing you're trying to hear and understand. Ask questions like "What made it seem that way?" or "How long have you felt this way?" or "How do I give you that impression?" or, simply, "Say a little more about that." Lastly, say something that shows you've been listening. Reflect what the person just said even if you don't agree and it makes you angry or frustrated: "So, you're saying I've never cared about you; that must be rough," or "I hear that you're really frustrated, makes sense," or "I guess you're telling me this again because I haven't shown you that I get it."

Show up. Attend healing and recovery events to which you've committed or are drawn to even when you are hungry, angry, lonely, or tired and prefer to stay home. Your problematic loved ones let their emotional states override their agreements and promises. Model the opposite. Show up for your recovery, your important relationships, what matters to you, and, most importantly, for your self-care and health.

Tell the truth. Don't be offended by this suggestion. The truth that needs to be told is often to oneself: "I'm at risk of doing my Classic right now," or "This really activates my belief I can't stand her discomfort." It's also important to endeavor to speak the truth about what's going on between you and another or inside you, employing the process and self-aware methods from communication practice. Examples from Dan's use of these principles in chapter 6: "I'm not up for doing more than we planned today," or "I'm feeling really churned up right now, let's take a break."

Ask for and use help. Like the illnesses plaguing the loved ones, your condition requires help. Seek others who "get it." Confide in someone qualified to help with your distress: clergy, therapists, mentors, experts, or fellow travelers as found in Al-Anon.

Build a network of allies and spend time with them. Like the situation facing your loved one(s), your dispiriting or desperate condition worsens in isolation. Maybe you sometimes speak with a spouse or partner or parent; however, these others, loving though they may be, cannot assist you in the same way as others who "get it" and have been there. Al-Anon family groups are filled with such people. Meetings are easy to find and always free to attend. Investigate six to ten of them in your area or online if you're in a rural area. In the meetings, look for those who have found freedom from the family condition as a result of doing the work in Al-Anon. When you work the Twelve Steps of Al-Anon with a sponsor, your recovery will soar to a level unavailable through any other method. Similar relief cannot be produced in isolation or with one or two others who are also embroiled in your situation.

Write, journal. Writing opens your mind in a way that can't be accessed by thinking alone. Try writing two to three pages each morning of whatever comes to mind. Your thoughts will begin to flow in a more natural way as you clear your mind of clutter and interfering or obsessive thoughts. When distressed by another's behavior or an unpleasant interaction, write about what they did, what it activated in you, what you did, what result you obtained, and what you could have done instead.

Pray, meditate. Quieting the mind is essential to produce serenity and becoming open to connection.[2] Readers of this book have been obsessing, ruminating, planning, analyzing, "snoopervising," keeping track, and repeating other mind-jumbling and confusion-inducing thinking patterns. Praying in this context can be thought of as asking for help to stop doing these things. Meditating involves listening for the answer. There are many books on mindfulness. See the selected bibliography at the end of the book for a few titles. Begin meditating by taking two minutes of quietly following your breath, or a five-minute guided meditation. There are online options to help you launch a simple meditation practice. A Google search for guided meditation produced 61,600,000 results in 0.37 seconds.

Improve self-care. Make a commitment to take better care of yourself. Most fixers, whether brokers, directors, or martyrs, have neglected their own needs for decades, likely since childhood. They've been conditioned on a deep level to put others' needs first. Fixers likely lost some ability to know what's best for themselves. Start with the basics: bathing; napping; caring for your skin, nails, hair (men too!); and exercise; even simply walking twenty to thirty minutes daily. Raise your game by adding massage, yoga, and an activity that gives you real pleasure such as cycling, kayaking, tennis, mahjongg, bridge club, book club, cooking class, photography, learning a new sport or language, or invigorating your sex life. Most importantly, make your needs the top priority.

WRAPPING IT ALL UP

When you've worked the SIIC recovery process to this point, you'll be able to describe the personal benefits obtained and see shifts toward wellness in your family system. The world you see will seem less insane, perhaps more serene. You'll have changed your belief system by uncovering the covert messages you received as a child and rejecting the lies that bind you in your relationships of today. The past slips away when you're no longer regretting it or obsessing over the impossible tasks others won't let you complete on their behalf. Seeking connection over being right, supported by mindfulness and self-awareness methods, makes it possible to "expand the sense of now and dissolve the fear."

Freedom from family dysfunction occurs when you can declare, "It stops with me." This captures your intention to interrupt the cycles of illness and loss in your family of today and on behalf of the next generation(s). You will have embraced William James's quote and fulfilled its promise:

> The world we see that seems so insane is the result of a belief system that is not working. To perceive the world differently, we must be willing to change our belief systems, let the past slip away, expand our sense of now, and dissolve the fear in our minds.

The next and final chapter is an overview of the SIIC model and the fundamental eleven steps of its recovery method. Addressing stress-induced impaired coping will interrupt the cycles of illness and loss that have repeated across the generations. Wellness and serenity for all family members become a real possibility. You will truly be able to declare, "It stops with me and I'm not going back."

· 9 ·

Freedom from Family Dysfunction

Staying on the Path

You can be transformed from quivering hostage walking on eggshells to architect of family serenity, safety, and sustainability.

$\mathcal{A}$nna and Brian's teenaged son James had so intruded into their relationship that on the evening before James entered drug and alcohol treatment, they didn't even appear to be a couple. Brian spent most evenings in the family room eating ice cream and falling asleep while watching violent TV. Anna spent hours on the phone with her girlfriends to distract herself from the pain and turmoil in her family.

Years later, Anna and Brian have successfully eliminated the disabling effects of Stress-Induced Impaired Coping. He runs a business; she's a successful yoga teacher and spiritual mentor. Their network of allies who helped them through the early days of their work have become dear friends.

James, now twenty-eight, has a fast-paced job, a loving wife, and a beautiful baby girl. James has a caring and fun-loving relationship with his parents. He said his parents' recovery was as necessary for him to get well as was his own treatment.

Anna and Brian's recovery path transformed them from estranged, held hostage, and burdened into a creative, loving couple. Along the way they examined their families of origin, described the family deal, identified the sticky beliefs they held, and shut down the "Fix James' Messes" business they had been caught in for nearly a decade.

"I am able to honor my own spiritual, mental, physical needs right alongside those of my husband," Anna said. "[In the family workshop], it was not fun to identify as a 'Fixer,' to look at my wounded and chaotic Family of Origin, and to see that I didn't know my own needs, much less have a voice to express them. Until I did the 'Lies That Bind' work, there was no way I would ever have said to anyone, 'I can't stand James's discomfort' or that I believed 'I owed him' from my troubled pregnancy. And I was very uncomfortable when I identified as a tidepool, my personal metaphor for what I'd become when things were at their worst. In that state, I was either drained dry or flooded, at the whim of forces completely outside my control, like the tides. My beliefs, fears, and projections kept me stuck and unable to see the truth."

Anna identified the methods she employed and the results she obtained to help her shift away from the "Fixer" role.

THE FUNDAMENTALS OF RECOVERY

The tools and skills in this book offer a gentle and compassionate way to touch your and your family's woundedness with love. As we recap them here, consider the work you have done so far and what you are willing to add or continue.

Here are the fundamental eleven steps of the SIIC recovery method:

1. Declare the current deal unsustainable and no longer okay.
2. Decide to no longer participate in that deal in exactly the same way.
3. Build a network of allies who "get it" to walk you through doing things differently.
4. Make an inventory of what you've tried.
5. List the results of your efforts including the evidence for their futility.
6. Figure out your own needs and preferences and insist on honoring them.
7. Create separation or move closer to family members.
8. Take small steps to promote serenity in your environment.
9. Use mindfulness practices to free yourself from beliefs that have kept things stuck.
10. Trust your loved ones to solve their problems.
11. Set everyone free to find their path—including you.

Let's summarize each step through the lens of Anna and Brian's story.

1. Declare the Current Deal Unsustainable

Years of accumulated pain and suffering had piled up to the day when Brian and Anna concluded that whatever they were doing to "help" James was not working. One rainy day, in the hallway of their suburban home, they looked at each other, defeated, and admitted that they no longer—singly or together——had the solutions for James.

The data were clear. James smoked a prodigious amount of marijuana nightly. He had just made a court appearance with costly legal fees for defacing private property. The high school continually threatened to kick him out because of his belligerent attitude. He was close to being suspended from the sports team where he had been a minor star. He had enlisted a host of girls to complete his homework in exchange for . . . well, Brian and Anna didn't want to know. Visits from or brushes with the law were becoming commonplace.

"I can't help him anymore," Brian told Anna quietly as they stood in the hall between James's room and their bedroom door.

Anna felt a stab of fear and high anxiety when Brian said this. "I knew what Brian said was true, but it was devastating to admit there was nothing I could do to change my son," she said.

They declared to each other right there: "This is not okay. If we keep on like this, we're going to lose everything, including our son." That began their journey from Classic caretaking and fixing toward healthy emotional detachment and, as an unexpected benefit, a reinvigorated marriage.

2. No Longer Participate in the Deal in the Same Way

Following their admission, Brian and Anna sent James to long-term, intensive treatment. They also made some key decisions about their communication: They would be in closer contact with each other, they would not collude with James on any "fix-it" or spending schemes, they would not take any action on James's behalf without consulting the other, and they would communicate openly with James's older sister about the entire situation.

Until he left with an interventionist to go to treatment, James continued to dog Brian for money and ask Anna for help with things she began to see he could do for himself. With each other's support, these were firmly but kindly refused. In addition, the parents dropped other Classic behaviors such as questioning their son about his activities or monitoring his whereabouts. A safer, more relaxed climate began to emerge in the household. Although James's behavior did not change much at this point, what he did or didn't do commanded less attention from his parents and therefore caused less turmoil.

3. Build a Network of Allies Who "Get It"

Following the hallway conversation, Brian and Anna contacted key potential helpers. Anna found a therapist, contacted a previous mentor, deepened contact with friends, and stopped listening to her mother's and sister's suggestions for James. Brian returned to individual therapy and went to some AA meetings to hear, as it was suggested, what people in recovery sound like and talk about.

The team at James's treatment center referred the parents to a parent support group. Increasing their support further, the couple began attending Al-Anon family groups in their area. There they were exposed to the power of Twelve-Step recovery for co-addicts or codependents. They met many parents and partners who were free of the bondage of living for someone else. Each eventually got an Al-Anon sponsor and worked its twelve steps.

In parent group, Anna and Brian heard others express fear of losing their child and admit to shame about not being able to solve things. As they began to share similarly, their feelings of shame and inadequacy diminished rapidly.

"It was like coming out of a fog," Anna said of her experience in the parent workshops and in Alanon. "The fixing was just the tip of the iceberg. I had a lot of work to do on me. I wouldn't have been able to admit all of the things I'd done—including keeping secrets from Brian— if I hadn't heard Al-Anon and parent group members sharing about such things," she added. "They helped me feel safe and get honest."

4. Make an Inventory of What You've Tried

The couple listed all the methods they'd tried—separately and together. Several were unknown to the other, as some of the caretaking had been kept secret. They were startled to discover how much energy, time, and effort they'd poured into The James Project. Between them they had tried bribing, blaming, lecturing, making appointments, taking away privileges and electronic devices, keeping secrets, and making absurd bargains like offering $100 for every A he earned in school.

Anna learned how her emotional beliefs, including "I can't stand his discomfort" and "I owe him," made it possible to repeat these futile efforts. She also recognized the power of her belief about what constitutes a "good mother." She coped with the divorce, mental illness, substance abuse, high anxiety, and codependence in her family of origin by being the super-helpful one. She repeated this with her children—secretary of the PTSA board, room mother, graduation party committee chair. When listing all the things she had tried to fix James, she saw how much of it was done in order to live up to this distorted standard of "good mother."

For his part, Brian saw how his wish for the bad times to be behind them kept him trying to fix things. He fed on the crumbs of James's brief successes or moments of apparent honesty to tell himself things were fine again.

5. List the Results of These Efforts

"It was painful for me to admit that my efforts to fix James's problems created a wedge between Brian and me . . . and they also served as a barrier from my own, true self," Anna said. "All the caring, worrying, and caregiving left me cut off from my integrity and myself."

Brian admitted he had become more depressed and reclusive. The couple also identified an increase in powerlessness as their efforts to fix became nearly obsessive. For James, results of his parents' efforts to change him included: increased marijuana use, anger, isolation, worsening grades, loss of friends and confidence, and trouble with the law.

6. Figure Out Your Needs and Preferences

Early in her recovery process, Anna had been encouraged to focus on her self-care. "I felt guilty about taking care of myself or having fun while James was in treatment," she said. Encouraged by therapists and Al-Anon fellows, she made a list of the things that soothed or excited her. "My hot tub was my savior," Anna said. "Until James went to treatment, I couldn't allow myself to slow down. My cover story was 'he needs me,' but, underneath, I believed that my sadness might consume me." She began a series of yoga classes and resumed her dormant watercolor painting passion. Brian bought a new bicycle and replied to an ad to join a band.

For many, this step is difficult. You have internal messages that caring for yourself is selfish, especially if someone who relies upon you is not doing well. The opposite is true, especially for your offspring. Children of any age want parents who live their lives fully. Recall the list of spiritual actions (recovery actions) offered in chapter 8. Determine which of those you might adopt. Go back to your teen and young adult years in your mind. Resume an activity you used to enjoy, especially if it involved being with others. Listen carefully to what other family members in recovery do to take care of themselves or have fun. As Nike says, "Just Do It."

7. Create Separation or Move Closer

Anna and Brian determined that separating James from their environment was necessary both for their own sanity and for him to have a real chance at getting well. After doing so, they came home to an empty nest. They were forced to look at each other and ask, "Do I know you? Do I want to spend time with you?" The years of focus on their son had created a gap between them that they hadn't noticed. And now the house was quiet—just the two of them alone with each other.

With many couples, the focus on a problematic child glues together a marriage that has gone otherwise lifeless and unexamined—often outside the awareness of either partner. Anna and Brian decided they would move toward each other, work to rebuild their marriage, and deepen their intimacy.

Move toward other children in the family, especially those who have seemed "fine" while the troubled one was out of control. The label "fine" is usually inaccurate. More likely, these fine ones have felt obliged not to add to the problems of the household, given the stress and strain caused by their high-profile sibling. They cut themselves off from knowing their needs. Drop the assumption they're fine and move in. In the same way as you're determining your own needs, help them identify theirs. Almost certainly, more time with you will be on their list. Rescue them from the invisibility resulting from being seen as "fine."

8. Take Small Steps to Promote Serenity

Identify one aspect of the family situation you feel ready to take up. It could be setting a single limit, such as "no smoking in the house," as the couple in chapter 8 employed. Another option might be to address spending, phone use, car sharing, or the delegation and performance of chores. Start small and with a belief that you can succeed. One tactic challenges parents to partner closely on a specific task, facing it together, without letting up, and backing each other up throughout.

Brian and Anna began with an effort to change the way they communicated with their son. The couple built on the success they had with this method to create closeness between them and healthier detachment from James's detail and drama.

"I came to understand that going forward with James, I needed to stop the 'Detective Mom' method and communicate with James and shift to using 'I' statements and talking about me. I studied nonviolent communication.[1] To prepare for phone calls and meetings with James, I did role plays about James with my therapist and my Al-Anon sponsor. I talked to Brian about what I wanted to say versus what I needed to say for my own serenity."

Anna was guided by some of the detachment-promoting phrases and introspection questions outlined in previous chapters:

- "I trust you have what you need to handle this."
- "I just want to be in connection. I don't care about being 'right' in this situation."
- "What's happening inside of me?"
- "What are my needs?"

In addition, she and Brian both used limit-setting language, including:

- "No."
- "That won't work for me."
- "I'm not ready to . . ."
- "This isn't fun for me."
- "I get it. You are going to _____."
- "This is probably going to be really hard for you."
- "We're focusing on our needs. I see why that would seem foreign to you."

Lastly, Anna shared a "motto" from Al-Anon that tickled her funny bone with its perfect truth: "Never lose an opportunity to keep your big mouth shut!"

9. Use Mindfulness Practices

The Lies That Bind worksheet presented in chapter 8 helps to loosen the grip exerted by the powerful stories that have held you in Classic ways of thinking and responding. Mindfulness methods underlie this type of process. For example, take a thought such as "She can't do this without me." Imagine throwing the thought out in front and above you, about three feet into space above your forehead. Look up at it and notice it in space rather than in you. Imagine yourself as separate from it and its power. Examine it for its truthfulness and its timing: "Is that really true? Why am I thinking that right now?" And more powerfully: "What if I did nothing even for a few minutes?" In this way you're much less at risk of being taken over by the thought. Mindfulness practitioners say: "You will no longer be the thought."[2] Instead, separate yourself from its power by tossing it out and away from you.

For Anna, the Lies That Bind work proved to be some of the most important.

"Just stating my belief, 'I can't stand his discomfort,' made me squirm. Then, encountering 'I owe' and its origins in my guilt over my tumultuous pregnancy with James allowed me to make sense of why I could keep secrets from my husband, cover up for and beg or bribe my son to get him to be different for all those years." As Anna unpacked these beliefs and their effect on her, their grip loosened and she obtained a newfound freedom.

Consult the selected bibliography at the back of the book for some titles referring to mindfulness and its many applications and techniques.

10. Trust Your Loved Ones to Solve Their Problems

In systems permeated by hostile and exaggerated dependency, family members become deeply conditioned to figure things out for their problematic loved ones. In turn, learned helplessness (explained in chapter 3) develops for the identified patient (IP). They struggle a little; you endeavor to fix it; they get relieved. The next time, you rush in sooner and they struggle less; you fix again; they're absolved from struggling; and so on. Eventually, any hint of struggle or uncertainty results in someone swooping in with suggestions, repairs, and rescues. This person becomes increasingly helpless, erasing any self-confidence. The person's own abilities and talents for solving the problem go untested, and the capacity to struggle is lost.

Interrupt this pattern by learning to tolerate loved ones' uncertainty and anxiety. Insist on uncovering reliable evidence to prove they can't do something before soothing or solving. Give them time to struggle, perhaps even to fail at first. Here's Anna's version:

"I had not trusted James for a very long time—since he was arrested in middle-school. I was shown that he had a whole secret life that I knew nothing about, despite my Mom Detective skills," Anna said.

"When he called me from his placement after wilderness treatment to tell me he'd graduated from high school, you could have knocked me over with a feather. I had lost touch with the idea that he was capable," Anna said.

James's counselors and teachers told Anna and Brian that James had plowed through his schoolwork to complete his diploma early. In addition, he would be starting community college soon.

"We learned to let James lead his life, stumble, feel the pain of his choices, and then ask for help if he needed it," Anna said.

James required three months of wilderness treatment and an academic year in secondary placement in order to reconnect with his competent self and rebuild his capacity to struggle. These superior abilities were likely intact for him throughout. When he was offered the opportunity to tap into his core strengths, to be relied upon as an essential team member, and to enjoy the benefits of contributing to his group, he regained confidence and hope. As parents and partners of people struggling similarly, we can support and encourage their return to competency, or we can dumb them down to the point of near total helplessness.

11. Set Everyone Free to Find Their Path—Including You

Tolerate and respect others' struggles, rather than trying to ease their discomfort or protect them from difficulty. Consider that disturbed family members may be giving expression to the woundedness in the system—perhaps going back a generation or two—and not simply showing that they're out of control, addicted, or mentally ill. Think of their need for intensive help as providing an invitation for the family to change. Imagine the power of saying to a problematic child or spouse, "You have provided the invitation for all of us to get well." I've seen scores of people in treatment light up after hearing this: "Hey! I'm the invitation not the problem." Keep in mind it is as wearying and desperate to be the problem one as it is to be the person reading this book who likely has been trying to fix that person for years or decades.

"I don't ever want to stop learning about myself. I am motivated to keep on working to expand my understanding and consciousness," Anna said. "I will attend support groups at every landmark in my life, and I see the critical importance of asking for help. Most of all, I want to show up for all of life's challenges standing in my truth and goodness."

"I don't have a superpower to know what's best for others," Anna said in a more relaxed moment. "My job is me, and now that I've begun to work on me, I see I've come a long way. I also know I have a long way to go," she added hopefully.

As I conclude this book, I want to encourage each of you—and all of us—to step into this healing work to radically shift toward wellness. The system *will* respond. Focusing on yourself will require encountering your own woundedness. Do so with allies and trusted others nearby. Know that you are not alone. Question everything you think and believe. Be present for all your relationships. Seek love and connection even with those who can't live or behave as you'd prefer. At the same time, insist on your own safety and the sustainability of your setup.

Remember our affirmation: "My serenity and quality of life will no longer be conditional on the behavior or mental health of anyone else, including my children or spouse."

Notes

CHAPTER 1. BELIEF SYSTEMS: UNCOVERING THE WOUNDED FAMILY SYSTEM

1. Mark Wolynn, *It Didn't Start with You: How Inherited Family Trauma Shapes Who We Are and How to End the Cycle* (New York: Viking, 2016), 22–30.

CHAPTER 3. LOOKING INSIDE: WHAT KEEPS US STUCK?

1. Christopher Petersen, Steven F. Maier, and Martin Seligman, *Learned Help-lessness: A Theory for the Age of Personal Control* (Oxford: Oxford University Press, 1995), 8.

CHAPTER 4. INTERGENERATIONAL INSANITY: THE IMPAIRED COPING MODEL

1. Mark Wolynn, *It Didn't Start with You: How Inherited Family Trauma Shapes Who We Are and How to End the Cycle* (New York: Viking, 2016), 6.

2. Claudia Black, *"It Will Never Happen to Me!" Children of Alcoholics: As Young-sters—Adolescents—Adults* (New York: Ballantine Books, 1987), 10.

3. Bill W., *Alcoholics Anonymous: The Story of How Many Thousands of Men and Women Have Recovered from Alcoholism* (New York: Alcoholics Anonymous World Services, 2001), 87.

CHAPTER 8. "I JUST WANT ~~THEM~~ TO BE HAPPY": *YOUR* RECOVERY ACTION PLAN

1. Bill W., *Alcoholics Anonymous: The Story of How Many Thousands of Men and Women Have Recovered from Alcoholism* (New York: Alcoholics Anonymous World Services, 2001), 87.

2. See Rick Hanson, *Buddha's Brain: The Practical Neuroscience of Happiness, Love and Wisdom* (Oakland: New Harbinger, 2009), 206.

CHAPTER 9. FREEDOM FROM FAMILY DYSFUNCTION: STAYING ON THE PATH

1. Marshall B. Rosenberg, *Nonviolent Communication: A Language of Life* (Encinitas, CA: Puddle Dancer Press, 2003), 6--8.

2. Daniel J. Siegel, *Mindsight: The New Science of Personal Transformation* (New York: Bantam Books, 2010), 79-102.

Selected Bibliography

Beattie, Melody. *Codependent No More*. Center City, MN: Hazelden Publishing, 1986.

Black, Claudia. *"It Will Never Happen to Me!" Children of Alcoholics: As Youngsters—Adolescents—Adults*. New York: Ballantine Books, 1987.

Bradshaw, John. *Bradshaw on the Family: A Revolutionary Way of Self-Discovery*. Deerfield Beach, FL: Health Communications, 1988.

Brown, Stephanie, and Virginia Lewis. *The Alcoholic Family in Recovery*. New York: Guilford, 2001.

Erickson, Erik H. *Childhood and Society*. New York: W.W. Norton, 1950.

———. *Identity and the Life Cycle*. New York: W.W. Norton, 1959.

Ginott, Haim G. *Between Parent and Child: Revised and Updated: The Bestselling Classic That Revolutionized Parent-Child Communication*. New York: Harmony, 2003.

Hanson, Rick. *Buddha's Brain: The Practical Neuroscience of Happiness, Love and Wisdom*. Oakland, CA: New Harbinger, 2009.

Harari, Yuval N. *Sapiens: A Brief History of Humankind*. New York: Harper, 2015.

Herzog, James. *Father Hunger: Explorations with Adults and Children*. Abingdon, UK: Routledge, 2001.

Kabat-Zinn, Jon. *Wherever You Go, There You Are: Mindfulness Meditation in Everyday Life*. New York: Hachette Publishing, 2005.

———. *Full Catastrophe Living: Using the Wisdom of Your Body and Mind to Face Stress, Pain, and Illness*. Revised edition. New York: Bantam, 2013.

Kornfield, Jack. *A Path with Heart: A Guide through the Perils and Promises of Spiritual Life*. New York: Bantam, 1993.

Petersen, Christopher, Steven F. Maier, and Martin Seligman. *Learned Helplessness: A Theory for the Age of Personal Control*. Oxford: Oxford University Press, 1995.

Reedy, Brad M. *The Journey of the Heroic Parent: Your Child's Struggle and the Road Home*. New York: Regan Arts, 2015.

Rosenberg, Marshall B. *Nonviolent Communication: A Language of Life*. Encinitas, CA: Puddle Dancer Press, 2003.

Siegel, Daniel J. *Mindsight: The New Science of Personal Transformation*. New York: Bantam Books, 2010.

W., Bill. *Alcoholics Anonymous: The Story of How Many Thousands of Men and Women Have Recovered from Alcoholism*. New York: Alcoholics Anonymous World Services, 2001.

Walant, Karen B. *Creating the Capacity for Attachment: Treating Addictions and the Alienated Self*. Northvale, NJ: Jason Aronson, Inc., 1995.

Wandzilak, Kristina, and Constance Curry. *The Lost Years: Surviving a Mother and Daughter's Worst Nightmare*. Santa Monica, CA: Jeffers Press, 2006.

Wolynn, Mark. *It Didn't Start with You: How Inherited Family Trauma Shapes Who We Are and How to End the Cycle*. New York: Viking, 2016.

Index

About the Author

Kenneth Perlmutter, PhD, a California-licensed clinical psychologist, has more than thirty years of experience working with individuals and families facing complex psychological and behavioral health disorders. He founded the Family Recovery Institute in 2008, where he sees individuals and families in his role as family systems psychologist. In addition, the Institute, now located in Marin County, offers family intensives and clinician training in family systems theory and treatment methods, employing Perlmutter's proprietary model of Stress-Induced Impaired Coping. Dr. Perlmutter has provided clinical leadership roles and designed/installed family programs for several national-level treatment programs and agencies. As a professional educator, he has served on the graduate faculty of San Francisco State University's Counseling Department and as associate professor of chemical dependency studies at Cal State, East Bay. He has taught courses covering development across the life span, psychopharmacology, family systems theory, human sexuality, theory and technique of counseling, treatment planning and documentation, and supervision. Perlmutter has provided keynote presentations and breakout workshops at most of the major addiction and behavioral health care treatment conferences, including US Journal Training, C4 Recovery Solutions, Foundations Recovery Network, Southwestern School of Behavioral Health, the Ben Franklin Institute, the Institute for Integral Studies, and the Thelma-McMillen Foundations lecture series. For the past two years he has had the privilege to conduct a four-day workshop for client families of the Rainbow Treatment Center on the White Mountain Apache Reservation in Northern Arizona. Dr. Perlmutter was appointed founding credential chair of the International Association of Family Addiction Professionals.

9 781538 121948